The Essentials of AutoCAD

Matthew M. Whiteacre

Texas A&M University

Third Edition

Revised Printing

KENDALL/HUNT PUBLISHING COMPANY

4050 Westmark Drive   Dubuque, Iowa 52002

Contents

Introduction

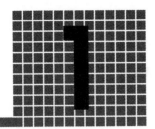

Background

Over the last two decades, computer graphics programs have come a long way. What used to be the realm of large super-computers, is now commonplace on home PC's. When the movie "The Last Starfighter" was produced in 1984, the animation was done strictly by computer; no models, no hand tweening, strictly on computer. This was the first movie to be so produced. The computer used was a Cray YMP and the cost was phenomenal. Today, Saturday morning cartoons can be produced on PC for a tiny fraction of the cost. There are many new programs that have been written during these two decades to meet the changing demands of industry and the public. One of the programs that has been around for the entire two decade period is AutoCAD.

AutoCAD was released in 1982 and was one of the first computer graphics programs to be written for a PC and marketed to a commercial environment. The initial release was crude by today's standards, but in 1982 the program was impressive. It was designed to allow professional draftsmen to create and edit drawings rapidly. The drawings were of the same nature the draftsmen had been working with, just the method to create them was different. Instead of picking up a pencil and paper, they executed the program on their PC and worked in that media. The concept of using a computer to do basic drawings was not new, but the concept of using a personal desktop computer to do it was very different.

AutoCAD did not try to design a program that was especially well suited for engineers, nor one that was especially tailored to architects; their goal was to make a simple to use generic program. They allowed third parties to develop software to compliment and enhance their basic program, thus you could get a separate module to draw structural steel, or windows and sofits, or landscaping contours, or piping design. You could even write your own enhancements for the software using a programming language called LISP. Using these basic concepts, AutoCAD gained a dominant place in the market and has held that place for 20 years. Today, of the people who use a personal computer drawing program to produce commercial 2D drawings, 70% of them use AutoCAD.

Purpose of This Book

The intention of this book is not to create expert users of AutoCAD. It is, instead, to provide an introduction to the basics of AutoCAD in a simple easy to follow manner. The sequence of instruction will have you up and using AutoCAD quickly, and will then build on the foundations as the book progresses. By the end of Chapter 2, you should feel comfortable getting into AutoCAD and doing a basic drawing. Some concepts, which are important in the long run, will be lightly brushed over initially to get you up and running. These concepts will then be re-examined in subsequent chapters to round out your abilities in AutoCAD.

What Is CAD?

Before beginning the study of a new program, it is important to realize what the purpose of the program is and how it can be applied. If you want to write a report on a subject, you want to use a word processor, not a spreadsheet. Likewise, if you want to create a drawing you use a drawing program, not a word processor. The problem is that there are many types of drawing programs with different focuses. Some focus on creating photo-realistic images, some on editing images, some on illustrations, and some on technical drawings. Each has a place in industry.

AutoCAD falls into the technical drawing category (actually if you use the 3D capabilities of AutoCAD, it can produce photo-realistic images). It will not apply bright, bold splashes of color on a drawing, instead it concentrates on allowing you to draw geometric figures (lines, circles, arcs, etc.) of precise size and then document, with dimensions, what you have drawn. Using this, you can lay out orthographic views of objects, draw pictorials, or even solve problems using descriptive geometry.

Conventions Used in this Book

While discussing actual AutoCAD commands in the text they will be listed in all caps, (i.e. LINE). Command streams will be shown in Courier font. The user input will be in boldface while directions will be shown italicized and enclosed in braces.

```
Command: offset
Specify offset distance or [Through] <1.0000>: 1/12
Select object to offset or <exit>: {select the circle}
Specify point on side to offset: {select a point inside the
    circle}
Select object to offset or <exit>:
```

Dedication

I would like to publicly thank several groups of people who have greatly assisted me in writing this book. First of all has to be my family, Jari, Monica, Sylvia, Alicia, John Paul, and Veronica, who put up with my being at the office many evenings and weekends to complete this book. Secondly is a group of friends, Mike, Jeff, and Jim, who help me make my deadlines by constant harassment about my progress. Without the support of either of these groups progress on the book would have been much slower and more painful than it was.

Getting A CLUE

Objectives

After completing this chapter, you should be able to:

1. Enter AutoCAD, exit AutoCAD, save a drawing file
2. Create drawings using Lines, Arcs, and Circles
3. Erase items from a drawing
4. Use the Undo command
5. Select items using either a normal window or a crossing window
6. Add text to a drawing using MTEXT or DTEXT

Beginning a New Drawing

After initially launching AutoCAD 2007, you will be presented with a startup dialog box shown in Figure 2.1. For two dimensional drawing you should select the AutoCAD Classic workspace. This textbook will assume you are working in the classic workspace.

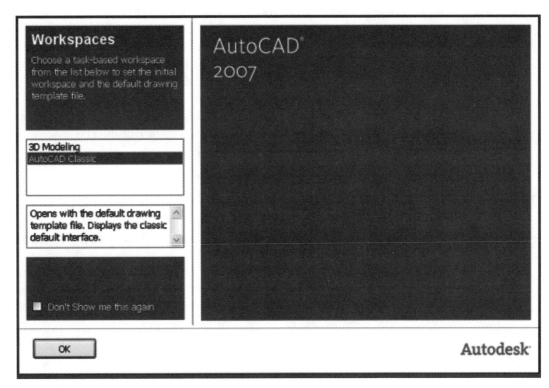

Figure 2.1

You should get a screen which looks like Figure 2.2.

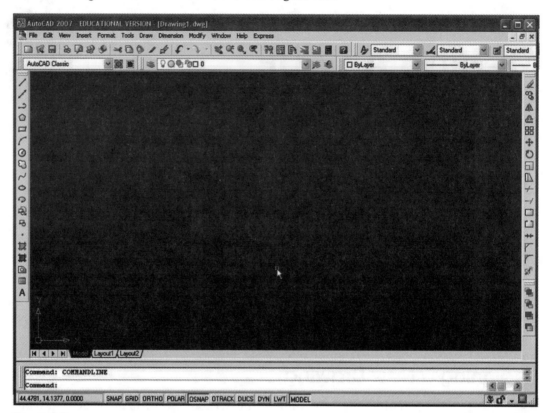

Figure 2.2

The majority of the screen is reserved for the actual creation of the drawing. The very top has pull down menus common to most Windows programs. The very bottom has a status line which shows what modes are active at the current time and the location of the cursor in X, Y, and Z. Just above this is the command prompt area where you can enter commands directly to AutoCAD. Set on the left edge and just above the drawing area are toolbars to facilitate drawing creation and editing.

Now that we have a drawing open, you can begin to add objects (the term AutoCAD uses for lines, arcs, etc.) to create a drawing. The normal method for adding objects to a drawing is by using the mouse, so we should examine the mouse before going any further.

Using the Mouse

Mice come in many different sizes and flavors, but the one reasonably common thing about them is that they all have at least 2 buttons, one labeled left and one labeled right. When using AutoCAD, the right button will be referred to as the right button and the left button is referred to as the pick button. The right button has the function of activating context sensitive menus or mimicking the function of the enter key, depending on what state AutoCAD is in at the time. The left button is used to pick icons, menu items, or points on the drawing area.

By placing the mouse over a toolbar icon and pressing pick (i.e. the left button), AutoCAD will activate the command associated with that icon; pressing the right button will activate a selection menu of all toolbars available in AutoCAD. The pulldown menus are activated using the left button. Point selection within the drawing area is made with the pick button, however, left clicking within the drawing area may also be used to select objects for editing. AutoCAD is context responsive to the needs of the user as it perceives them.

Actually Creating a Drawing

The toolbar on the far left edge of the screen is the Drawing toolbar. Figure 2.3 shows this with the buttons labeled. For this chapter, we are going to focus on the basic four commands: Line, Circle, Arc, and MText. The basic purpose of each of these commands should be readily identifiable, but a brief look at how AutoCAD implements them will be useful.

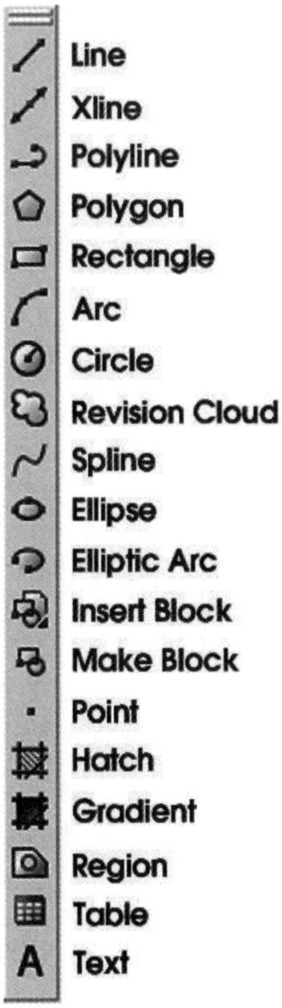

Drawing Lines

The line command allows you to draw independent straight line segments from point to point in AutoCAD. Once a line segment is created it becomes an object and can be manipulated independently from any other object on the screen. The command used to execute the line command is LINE if you are typing commands via the keyboard, or the alias L can be used also. Each line segment end point will be selected using the left mouse button (the pick button). A session would look like:

```
Command: line
Specify first point:
Specify next point or [Undo]:
Specify next point or [Undo]:
Specify next point or [Close/Undo]:
Specify next point or [Close/Undo]:
Specify next point or [Close/Undo]:
Specify next point or [Close/Undo]:
```

/	Line
/	Xline
↲	Polyline
⬠	Polygon
▭	Rectangle
⌒	Arc
⊘	Circle
☁	Revision Cloud
∿	Spline
○	Ellipse
◠	Elliptic Arc
⊡	Insert Block
⊡	Make Block
·	Point
▨	Hatch
▤	Gradient
◎	Region
▦	Table
A	Text

Figure 2.3

Notice that for the fourth and subsequent points, AutoCAD offered the option "Close." Using that option will draw another line segment from the previous point to the point selected as the "First point:" for the current set of line segments. To use that option you must type "Close" or "C" through the keyboard and press enter.

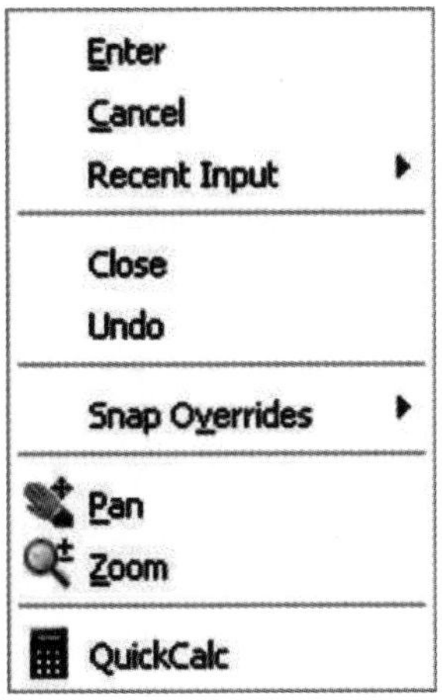

Enter
Cancel
Recent Input ▶
Close
Undo
Snap Overrides ▶
Pan
Zoom
QuickCalc

Figure 2.4

The other option available is "Undo" or "U" which will unselect the previous point and allow you to place it in the correct location. There are no limits on the number of times you may use the undo option. You could undo all the selections back to the "First point:" prompt if you wanted to.

To stop drawing lines with the current command you must press Enter or Escape to terminate the current command. When you do this, AutoCAD will return to the "Command:" prompt awaiting further instructions.

To access all those options with the mouse, right click during the line command and AutoCAD will display the popup menu shown in Figure 2.4. From here you may select any of the options listed above, or execute a Pan or Zoom operation. These will be discussed in Chapter 4.

Drawing Circles

The circle command allows you to draw circles in a variety of ways. The most common form requests a center point and the radius of the circle. With this information, AutoCAD draws the circle and terminates the command, returning to the "Command:" prompt. To use the command through the keyboard type "Circle" or "C" and press enter.

```
Command: c CIRCLE
Specify center point for circle or [3P/2P/Ttr (tan tan radius)]:
Specify radius of circle or [Diameter]:

Command: CIRCLE
Specify center point for circle or [3P/2P/Ttr (tan tan radius)]:
Specify radius of circle or [Diameter] <0.9059>: D
Specify diameter of circle <1.8117>: 3.25
```

In the above set of commands, the first set simply used the defaults and draws a circle using the center point and radius as selected by the left mouse button. The second circle selects the center point with the mouse, but utilizes the keyboard to specify that the diameter should be used and then that diameter is typed via the keyboard.

The other options that exist for circles are:

3Point—allows you to select any three non-colinear points and draws a circle through those points

2Point—allows you to specify two points along a diameter of a circle and draws the circle

TTR (tan tan radius)—does not ask for points to locate the circle, but two objects already drawn on the screen. A circle will be drawn tangent to those two objects with a specified radius (if the resulting circle does not exist, the AutoCAD will ignore it and will go back to the command prompt).

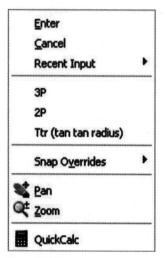

As with the Line command, you may right click and get a popup menu (Figure 2.5) to select the various options from.

Figure 2.5

Drawing of Arcs

Drawing arcs in AutoCAD requires a little more planning than either lines or circles. There are many more options for creating arcs than for lines and circles combined. Given this, we will explore another method to select commands in AutoCAD, the pulldown menus.

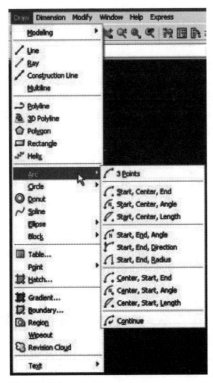

Figure 2.6

Under the Draw pulldown, you can select lines or circles, however these are easily drawn using the icons. Arcs present more of a challenge, since in normal engineering drawing, the default selection via the icon (a 3 point arc) is not the most common. The pulldown menu for drawing arcs is shown in Figure 2.6. The options available, in various combinations are:

Start: The point at which the arc should start.

Center: The center point of the arc.

End: The end point of the arc.

Angle: The total angle included in the arc.

Length: The length of the chord defined by the arc. This is not arc length, but chordal length.

Direction: The tangent direction for the arc at the start point.

Radius: The radius of the arc.

Arcs are always drawn counterclockwise in AutoCAD. If you want to draw an arc clockwise, you must use the Angle option and specify a negative angle. Figure 2.7 shows various options of the arc command.

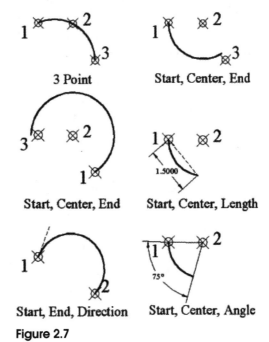

Figure 2.7

Using these three commands there are many things you can draw, but this is just a glimpse of the full power of AutoCAD. The ability to draw/create items in a CAD system is secondary to the ability to edit and make corrections. That is where the true power of a computer aided design system lies.

Erasing Unwanted Objects

To erase an object from the drawing you must invoke the ERASE command. The command is ERASE, or E is sufficient or pick the ERASE icon. Once you are using the command, the prompt in the command area will change to "Select objects:" and the crosshairs will change to a small square, indicating that you should pick (using the left mouse button) the objects you wish to delete from the drawing. As you select an object, it will highlight (become fuzzy looking). Once you have selected all the objects you wish to erase, complete the command by pressing the right mouse button or the enter button on the keyboard.

The "Select objects" prompt is very common in AutoCAD and offers many methods for forming *Selection Sets*. A Selection set is a collection of objects that are to be acted on by a given command. Initially, three options of the selection objects prompt will be examined: object picking, Window, and Crossing.

Object Picking requires that you place the small square cursor over an object and press the left mouse button. It will select one object and only one object. In order to select more than one item, you should use the Window or Crossing option. To access these options, place the square cursor on a portion of the screen without an object and press the left mouse button. AutoCAD will respond by telling you to "Specify opposite corner:" of a rectangular region. This region will either be a Window area or a Crossing area depending on your next action. By moving the mouse to the right or left of the initial selection point (vertical motion does not matter) you can switch from a Window to a Crossing. Windows are to the right and Crossings are to the left. You will notice that the rectangular area will switch from a solid rectangle to a dotted rectangle to illustrate the shift from Window to Crossing.

If you choose a Window area, then all objects which are completely enclosed by the rectangular region will be selected. While a Crossing area will select all those objects completely within the rectangle, it also selects those which touch the area at any point. In Figure 2.8 below, if the area being selected was a window, then the line and arc would be selected, but not the circle; if it were a crossing, then all three objects would be selected.

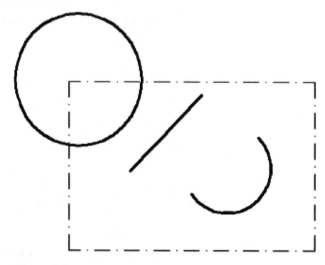

Figure 2.8

To remove an object from the selection before completing the erase, hold the shift key down while making a selection. This will unhighlight those objects.

Undoing an Action

AutoCAD, like most Windows programs, has a command specifically designed to give you an escape route when you have just done something you really didn't want to do: the Undo command. The icon is located on the upper toolbar or through the keyboard the command is "U" and it will reverse the last action taken. By using "U" multiple times you can, in theory, undo your entire drawing session. The UNDO list begins when you open a drawing, so any modifications you made during the previous drawing session cannot be undone.

Adding Text to a Drawing

The final tool that should be discussed for creating very simple drawings is text. Adding text to a drawing allows you to label the drawing as yours and to put explanatory notes on the drawing. There are two primary methods to apply text using AutoCAD: DTEXT and MTEXT.

DTEXT

DTEXT stands for Dynamic TEXT and, by today's standards, does not seem all that dynamic. The original text command (which can still be invoked by typing TEXT at the command prompt) required you to type your text at the command line, and upon completion the text would be displayed on the drawing. With Dynamic text the text appears on the drawing while you are typing it. It does not do any automatic word wrap, but you can see when you need to hit return to begin a new line of text. Each line so created is a separate object in AutoCAD. A sample session using DTEXT is shown below.

```
Command: dtext

Current text style: "Standard" Text height: 0.2000
Specify start point of text or [Justify/Style]:
Specify height <0.2000>: .125

Specify rotation angle of text <0>:

Enter text: This is the first line of text.
Enter text: The height was set to 1/8"
Enter text: This is engineering standard text height
Enter text:
Command:
```

To complete the command, press Enter without entering any text on that line. This will finalize the text created so far in the command and return you to the Command prompt. As you complete each line of text it is entered into the drawing. The font can be changed by modifying the text style. This will be discussed in Chapter 6.

If you select the Justify option, you can control the alignment of the text relative to the insertion point you selected. The various options are shown in Figure 2.9.

Left Justified Text	TR Justified Text
Center Justified Text	ML Justified Text
Right Justified Text	MC Justified Text
Middle Justified Text	MR Justified Text
TL Justified Text	BL Justified Text
TC Justified Text	BC Justified Text

Fit text option

Aligned text option

Figure 2.9

Rotation angle is relative to the X-axis. Some of the various choices are shown in Figure 2.10.

This is text at 90°

This is text at 120°

This is text at 60°

This is text at 150°

This is text at 30°

This is text at 180°

This is text at 0°

This is text at 210°

This is text at 330°

This is text at 240°

This is text at 270°

This is text at 300°

Figure 2.10

MTEXT

A

MTEXT stands for Multiline TEXT. The alias "T" will invoke it or it can be selected using the icon on the Drawing Toolbar. It is, in essence, a small built in word processor inside of AutoCAD. Upon invoking the MTEXT command, AutoCAD will ask you about locating the text on the drawing and then open a dialog box to allow you to type your text. The dialog box is very close to a WYSIWYG editor, including **Bold**, *Italic*, <u>Underline</u> and other special formatting. The command sequence is shown below, followed by the dialog box (Figure 2.11) with some text already typed.

```
Command: mtext
Current text style: "Standard" Text height: 0.1250
Specify first corner:
Specify opposite corner or [Height/Justify/Line spacing/
        Rotation/Style/Width]:
```

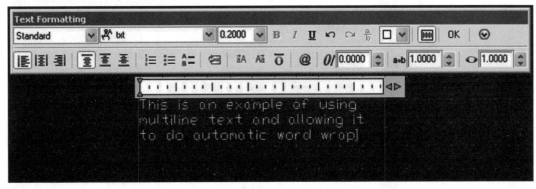

Figure 2.11

Depending on the font selected, different options will be available. The default font TXT is a very plain simple font designed for quick display. It has few options available. One of the options which is of interest to engineers is the ability to insert some standard engineering symbols. These are:

Ø—the diameter sign ← %%C

°—the degrees sign ← %%D

±—the plus/minus sign ← %%P

The %% codes can be used directly to place a symbol in a text string (these also work with DTEXT).

Alternatively, there are many standard symbols via Unicode. Many of these can be directly placed by selecting the down arrow on the MTEXT command bar as shown in Figure 2.12.

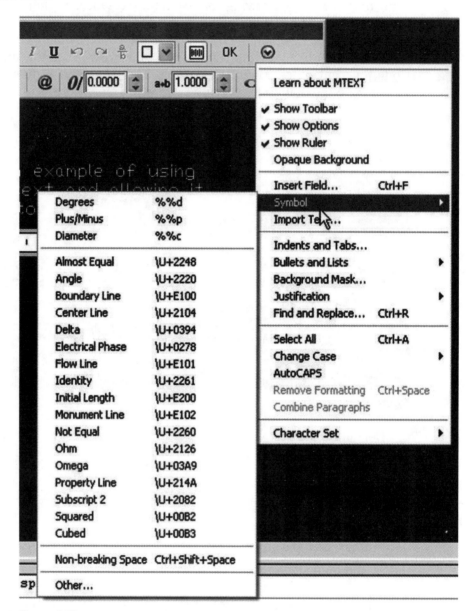

Figure 2.12

Saving a Drawing

Now that you have completed a drawing, you will probably want to save that drawing to disk for later retrieval. The basic command to do this is the SAVE command. The SAVE command will open a dialog box and ask you to name your drawing. If it is already named, the dialog box will still open and you will be allowed to change the name of the file (without disturbing the old file). The dialog box is shown in Figure 2.13. It is a standard Windows style save dialog box (this makes it somewhat dependent on the version of Windows you are using).

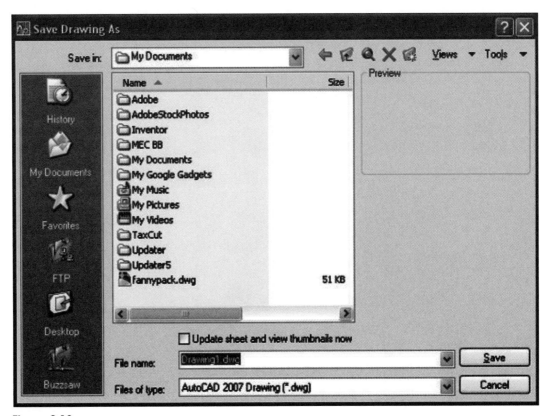

Figure 2.13

If you do not like having to reenter the filename each time you can use the QSAVE command (which is actually the command used by the icon for saving a file).

A Bit About the Title of the Chapter

This chapter is titled "Getting A CLUE." The phrase "ACLUE" is an easy acronym for remembering the keyboard shortcuts to the first five commands described in the chapter: **A**rc **C**ircle **L**ine **U**ndo **E**rase. You will find that it is frequently easier to use the keyboard shortcuts with your non-mouse hand than it is to run the mouse over to the appropriate toolbar and select an icon or to use the pulldown menus.

Review Questions

1. The status line is located at the top of the screen? True/False

2. Pressing the right mouse button will frequently invoke a context sensitive menu? True/False

3. The line segments created with the LINE command are linked and form one object in AutoCAD. True/False

4. What is the command alias (keyboard shortcut) for each of the following commands?

   Line   L

   Circle   C

   Arc   A

   Mtext   M

   Erase   E

5. While in the LINE command, entering "C" in response to a "next point" prompt will

   A) draw a circle tangent to the previous line segment.
   B) cancel the command.
   C) continue the line command from the previous point.
   D) draw a line segment from the current point to the beginning point for that line command.
   E) none of the above.

6. By default, the CIRCLE command expects a center point and

   A) radius.
   B) diameter.
   C) circumference.
   D) cord length.
   E) none of the above.

7. AutoCAD will allow you to draw a circle by specifying two points which lie on the circumference of the circle on opposite sides of a diameter. True/False

8. By default, arcs are drawn in a counterclockwise direction. True/False

9. The length option for an arc specifies the arc length for the resulting arc. True/False

10. When selecting objects, a dotted rectangle for a selection area is a crossing selection and will select the objects both inside and touching the rectangular area. True/False

11. The U command is limited to reversing the last 16 commands. True/False

15

12. Which of the following commands is not a valid AutoCAD command to place text on a drawing?

- A) TEXT
- B) DTEXT
- C) MTEXT
- D) VTEXT
- E) Both A and D

13. The DTEXT command creates individual lines of text while the MEXT command creates paragraphs. True/False

14. Which of the following text strings yields the diameter Ø sign?

- A) %%C
- B) %%D
- C) %%P
- D) %%T
- E) None of the above

Basic Settings in AutoCAD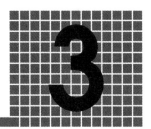

Objectives

1. Understand the importance of grid and snap
2. Understand the function of ortho and polar
3. Be able to control the size of the crosshairs on screen
4. Be able to use multiple layers in a drawing
5. Be able to use Template files
6. Be able to use Object Snap
7. Use the Standard layer Structure
8. Know how to set the correct Line Weights for engineering drawings
9. Be able to activate new toolbars

Grid and Snap

Grid and snap are actually very different items in AutoCAD. Both can be controlled through the status line at the bottom of the AutoCAD screen (shown in Figure 3.1). In the example shown, Snap is activated (referred to as turned on) and Grid is turned off. The state of either can be controlled by clicking on their button.

| 6.0000, 2.0000 , 0.0000 | SNAP GRID ORTHO POLAR OSNAP OTRACK DUCS DYN LWT MODEL |

Figure 3.1

In the final analysis, grid is not a critical concept and many people do not even use grid while drawing. Grid is simply the background set of dots that AutoCAD presents to assist you in measuring distances. The grid will not print. If you want a background grid on your prints, then special measures must be taken to draw that grid in AutoCAD.

Snap, on the other hand, is one of the most critical concepts for a beginning user of AutoCAD. Snap is a translation device that allows a computer and a human to speak on equal terms about precision drawing. The computer would prefer to think all input was accurate to 8 or more significant digits, while a human, looking at a standard monitor, would have trouble getting more than 3 significant digits (there are about 1000 pixels across a standard screen). By judicious setting of snap, this problem can be overcome. Snap requires that the cursor lock in at specific intervals.

Initially, this gives an uncomfortable feeling since the crosshairs on AutoCAD seem to jump from point to point (they really do jump). You are left with the question, what happens if I need to select a point which is not on a snap interval? You can either type the exact X and Y value through the keyboard or change snap to a more convenient interval. A common error beginning students make is to turn snap off to select a point and then forget to turn it back on. A good operating principle is DO NOT **DRAW** ANYTHING WITH SNAP TURNED OFF. When editing a drawing (using Erase, for instance) turning snap off is perfectly acceptable, just remember to turn it back on before drawing.

Some people who read the preceding paragraph will question the use of snap. For an experienced person in AutoCAD, snap is not a requirement. If you choose to not use snap, you must use some other means of insuring the accuracy of your drawing. These do exist, but are more cumbersome to learn initially, thus the basic statement "DO NOT DRAW ANYTHING WITH SNAP TURNED OFF" still stands for beginning students.

To control the setting of either Snap or Grid, you should right click on either button and select the Settings option from the popup menu displayed. This will activate the Drafting Settings dialog box shown in Figure 3.2.

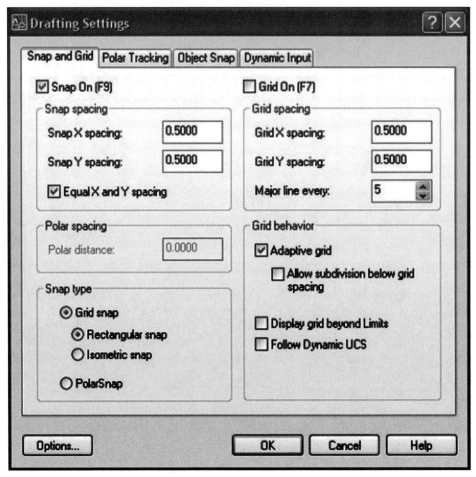

Figure 3.2

You may change either setting by modifying the value shown in the dialog box. Alternatively, you can type the command GRID or SNAP in at the Command: prompt and modify the value through the keyboard. If you modify the "X" value for either grid or snap, the "Y" value will be set equal to the "X," however, if you modify the "Y" value, the "X" remains unchanged, thus allowing you to have different "X" and "Y" increments.

Use of Ortho

Right next to the Grid and Snap buttons on the status line is a button labeled ortho. This is a special mode AutoCAD uses to restrict the location of point selection when drawing objects. If activated, after the initial point is selected, subsequent points are restricted to being directly above, below, to the right or left of the previous point. This allows you to draw stair steps with line segments, but not ski slopes. It can be turned on or off at any time by left clicking on the button labeled ORTHO.

Use of Polar

Similar to Ortho, Polar allows you to draw lines at predetermined angles. It is mutually exclusive with Ortho, so only one of them can be active at any time. By default the angles for Polar are set at 90 degrees. Even at this setting Polar has advantages over Ortho. With Polar, the crosshairs will not be forced to constrain themselves to the fixed angles, but will lock in to the angles when the crosshairs get within 3 degrees of the angle settings. When they lock in on an angle, the display will show the distance from the previous point and the angle as shown in Figure 3.3. If you

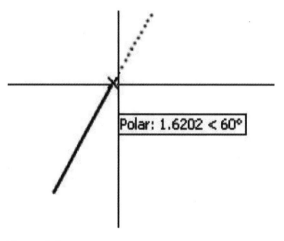

Figure 3.3

have both Snap and Polar activated, then the point selected will be on the polar angle, even if that means pulling it off a snap point. One useful tool to use in conjunction with Polar is Polar Snap (see the lower right quadrant of Figure 3.2). Polar Snap will snap to fixed increments along the pre-set polar angles.

To activate Polar, pick the button labeled "Polar" at the bottom of the screen. This will activate Polar, and deactivate "Ortho" (if it was on). The angles will be set to whatever was last used on the computer. To set the angles, right click on the "Polar" button and select settings. The following dialog box will be displayed (Figure 3.4). To

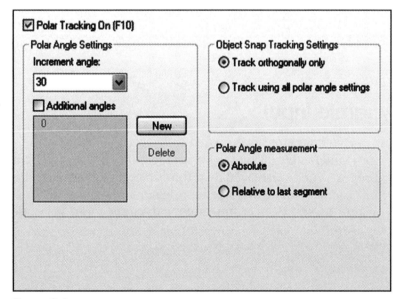

Figure 3.4

change the angle settings, drop down the "Increment angle:" box and select the new increment. In the box shown in Figure 3.4, the crosshairs will lock at 0°, 30°, 60°, 90°, etc. If you want to include any angles which are not multiples of the increment, they must be added to the list of additional angles.

To add a 45° to the above setting, select the New button and type the additional angle on the list of angles. The new box should look like Figure 3.5 which shows the additional angle of 45°. Note that this does not add 135°, 225°, or 315°. These would have to be added separately, if needed.

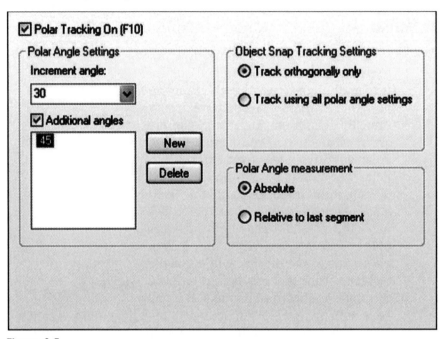

Figure 3.5

Resizing the Crosshairs

When AutoCAD is installed, the default size for the crosshairs covers only 5% of the screen. Many designers prefer crosshairs which span the entire screen. The size of the crosshairs is controlled by a setting called CURSORSIZE. This parameter represents the size of the crosshairs, in percent of screen size. To reset the size, simply type CURSORSIZE in response to the Command: prompt and type the desired value.

```
Command: cursorsize
Enter new value for CURSORSIZE <5>: 100
```

Use of Dynamic Input

Dynamic input is designed to keep your focus on the drawing area by providing basic interactive text at the cursor location. If you type a command from the keyboard the text will be displayed near the cursor, if you are in a command, location, distance, or prompts will be displayed at the cursor location rather than on the command line. Figure 3.6 shows an example of the dynamic input associated with the line command.

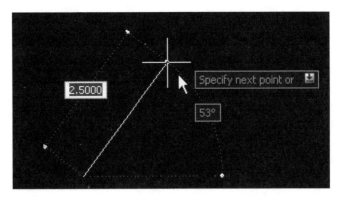

Figure 3.6

Use of Layers

While snap is one of the most important concepts while using a CAD system, layers are at about the same importance level. Using layers correctly will make it easier to work on large projects, especially those projects done by a team of engineers. Layers are a sorting system used by AutoCAD to keep track of objects and to categorize them based on the function they have within the drawing. Some lines are visible lines; some are construction lines. By identifying the function of the object to AutoCAD, it will correctly set the parameters associated with that type of line (i.e., don't print construction lines, print visible lines bold, draw hidden lines with dashes, etc.).

In this course, you should not have to create your own layers since the base templates (see later in this chapter) for the workbook have been created and are available on your computer in the classroom. Appendix 7 will discuss the creation of template files should you need to build your own in the future. For now, there are only two things you need to know about the mechanics of layers: how to switch from one to another and how to turn them on or off.

These two operations can be performed by using the dropdown layer selection box on the object properties toolbar shown in Figure 3.7 (the lower toolbar at the top of the screen). It will always display the name of a layer created in the current drawing if you are trying to draw an object. All objects must reside on a layer, they cannot be left "floating" and layerless. The layer on which they are drawn determines several properties of the object. These include: color, linetype, and lineweight. These parameters can be controlled individually for objects, regardless of layer, BUT THIS IS HIGHLY DISCOURAGED FOR BEGINNING STUDENTS. The three boxes to the right of layer name should be left as BYLAYER, thus allowing all objects to inherit their properties from the layer on which they are created.

Figure 3.7

To change from one layer to another you must drop down the list of layers and select a new one from the resulting list by clicking on the name of the layer. The layer visible will be the new current layer if the selection button was pressed while it is highlighted as shown in Figure 3.8.

To turn a layer on or off (it is a toggle) drop down the same list

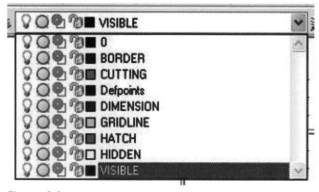

Figure 3.8

and left click on the light bulb to the far left of the layer name. It will switch from bright (yellow) to dim (gray) or vice versa. Turning the layer off will suppress the display of the objects drawn on that layer, without erasing them from the drawing.

Limits

Limits are set in AutoCAD to allow the drawer to have a reserved area to draw in. They set the theoretical edges of the paper and help maintain perspective when drawing. The grid will only show within the limit defined in the drawing. To change the limits set for a drawing, use the command LIMITS and enter, via the keyboard, the lower left and upper right coordinates to define the page size.

Line Weights

Line weight refers to how wide a line is drawn when it is printed. It does not necessarily affect the way a drawing is displayed on the screen. You can turn on line weight display by clicking on the LWT button on the status line. This is a rough approximation of the plotted output, but is occasionally useful.

Figure 3.9 shows an example of line weights. When printing engineering drawings it is important to use the correct line weights for each line type. Table 3.1 shows the most common line types and the recommended sizes for each as per ANSI standards.

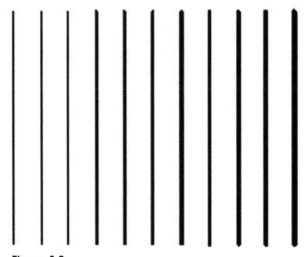

Figure 3.9

Table 3.1 Common Line Weights		
Line type	Width (inches)	Width (mm)
Visible	0.02	0.5
Hidden	0.014	0.35
Center	0.01	0.25
Cross Hatching	0.01	0.25
Cutting Plane	0.028	0.7
Dimension	0.01	0.25

If your line weights are not set correctly, use the command LAYER to assign a line weight to a layer.

Template Files

Template files are designed to allow companies or individuals to store predefined configurations for drawings. They preset many of the settings discussed in this chapter, thus allowing the CAD operator to begin drawing immediately, rather than take time to set up everything for each drawing. They can also include standard drawn objects, like a border or company logo.

For this class, template files allow your instructor to make copies of the basic setting needed to complete each drawing on your computer, thus relieving you of a lot of overhead required to start all drawings from scratch.

Object Snap

While snap is a very useful tool, there are times when you really need to draw to a point which is not on a snap point, and it might be very difficult to find exactly the snap you needed to force it on a snap point. One example is to draw a 3 point arc, then draw a line from the center of that arc to each of the end points.

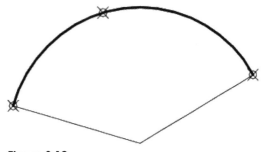

Figure 3.10

The chances that the center point will fall exactly on a snap point are slim to none. However, AutoCAD has an additional snap mode called object snap, OSNAP, to allow the user to lock onto points which are referenced by objects in the drawing by simply getting the crosshairs close to the desired locations. There are two different modes available for OSNAP, running and override. Running OSNAP is really a setting for AutoCAD, override is just a one point effect and it will be discussed only because it relates so closely to running osnap.

To activate running osnap select the button labeled OSNAP at the bottom of the screen. The first time you do this you will be presented with a dialog box of available options as shown in Figure 3.11. Each subsequent time the button will either activate

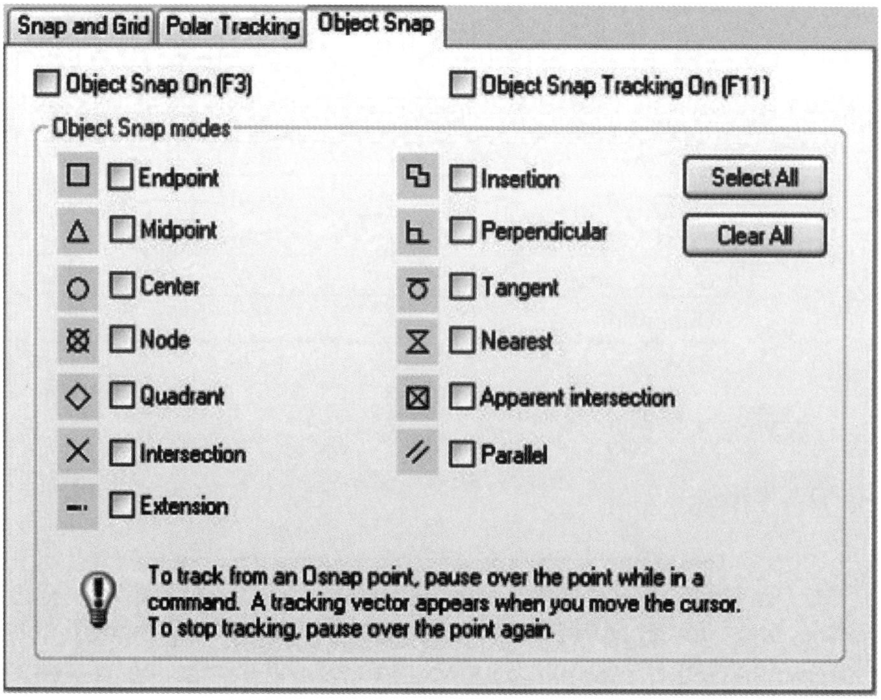

Figure 3.11

or deactivate the options you choose on this dialog box. If you want to see this box in the future, you must right click on the button and select settings.

Some of the various modes are:

Endpoint: This will choose the end points of an arc or line.

Midpoint: This will choose a point on an arc or line that is exactly in the middle. For an arc this is NOT the center point of the arc, it lies on the arc at its middle.

Center: The center of arcs or circles.

Quadrant: One of the points on an arc or circle which is at 3 o'clock, 6 o'clock, 9 o'clock, or 12 o'clock.

Intersection: The physical intersection between two objects. You may pick one object and then the second or locate the crosshairs over the intersection point and make your selection.

Insertion: The reference point for text.

Perpendicular: Selects a point on the object where a line perpendicular to the object and passing through the previous point (used in this command) would be. If this is the first point requested by the current command, it will allow a deferred perpendicular, which will not select the first point (the one on the object) until the next point is chosen. It then back calculates where the perpendicular needs to be and selects that point.

Tangent: Selects a point to allow the line, arc, or circle to be tangent to a selected arc or circle. Like the perpendicular option, this can be used in deferred mode to allow you to draw something tangent to an object and perpendicular to another.

Once you have selected the modes you would like to use, select the OK button and return to the drawing. The next time AutoCAD requests a point, it will try to observe the object snap rules you have established. If no point matches your osnap criteria, then it will select a point normally. If multiple points match the criteria, the AutoCAD will select the one closest to the actual crosshair location. If you want another possible selection, then pressing the tab key will cycle through all the available options.

The second mode, override osnap, functions exactly as running osnap except it is good for only one point selection, then the system reverts back to the running osnap settings. To use this option you may type the osnap mode in via the keyboard (the first three letters are sufficient) or select the icon from the dropdown toolbar icon shown in Figure 3.12. The one additional setting that is available for override osnap is "none" which cancels any running osnap modes for the next point selection. These can also be accessed from the popup menu under the Snap Overrides section as shown in Figure 3.13.

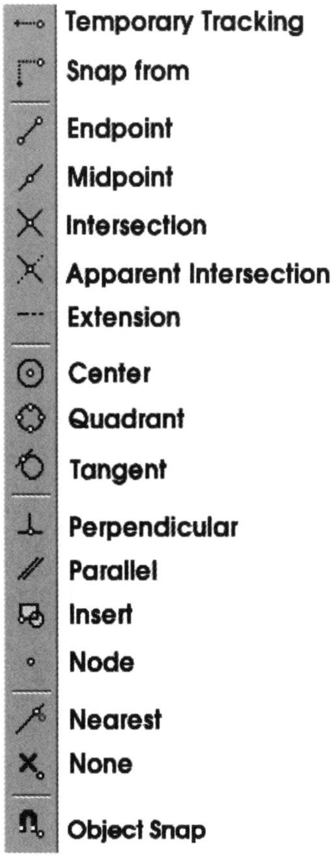
Temporary Tracking
Snap from
Endpoint
Midpoint
Intersection
Apparent Intersection
Extension
Center
Quadrant
Tangent
Perpendicular
Parallel
Insert
Node
Nearest
None
Object Snap
Figure 3.12

One closely related option is Object Snap Tracking. Beginning students should probably just make sure OTRACK (on the button bar at the bottom of the screen) is turned off. It will cause AutoCAD to create temporary tracking points using the OSNAP and polar angle snap settings. There are some very useful things which can be done with OTRACK, but it tends to be confusing to the beginning student.

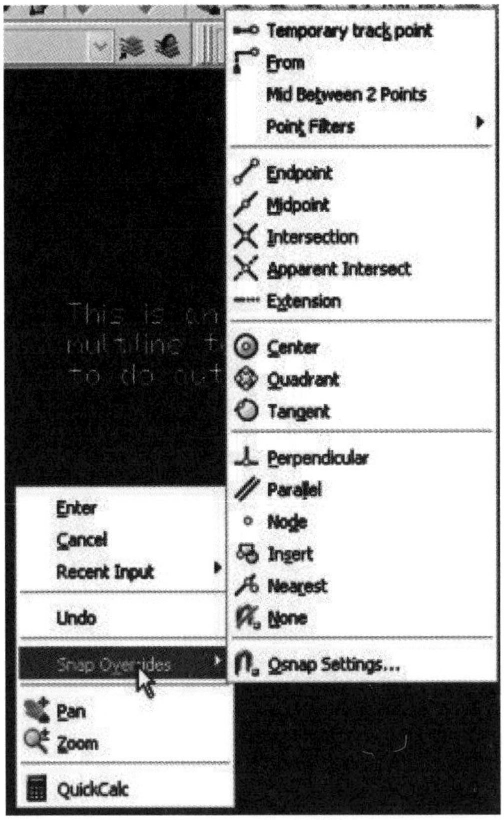
Temporary track point
From
Mid Between 2 Points
Point Filters
Endpoint
Midpoint
Intersection
Apparent Intersect
Extension
Center
Quadrant
Tangent
Perpendicular
Parallel
Node
Insert
Nearest
None
Osnap Settings...
Enter
Cancel
Recent Input
Undo
Snap Overrides
Pan
Zoom
QuickCalc
Figure 3.13

Activating Toolbars

AutoCAD comes with 35 different toolbars available, fortunately they are not all displayed on the screen at the same time. If they were, the screen would look like Figure 3.14.

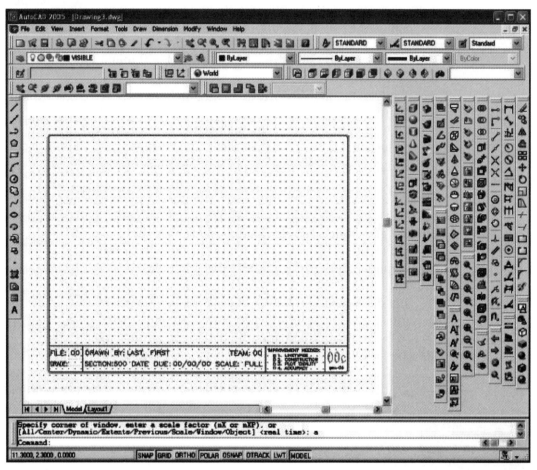

Figure 3.14

If you would like to open a toolbar which is not visible, you may right click on any existing toolbar and select the new toolbar from the resulting popup menu. If no toolbars are visible, then you can use the pulldown menu VIEW → Toolbars . . . to activate them. When AutoCAD first loads, the following toolbars are normally visible on the screen: "Standard Toolbar" and "Object Properties" at the top and Draw and Modify on the side. If, for some reason, you do not have these visible, you may reactivate them and drag them into place.

Review Questions

1. You should remember to turn GRID off before printing your drawing.
   True/False

2. What is the maximum precision possible for the human eye on most computer monitors?

   A) 2 significant digits
   B) 3 significant digits
   C) 5 significant digits
   D) 8 significant digits
   E) The monitor has nothing to do with it

3. AutoCAD will allow you to set the X and Y values for SNAP to different values.
   True/False

4. If AutoCAD will not allow you to draw diagonal lines, what mode do you most likely have active?

   A) Polar
   B) Snap
   C) Ortho
   D) Grid
   E) Fixed

5. What mode will display the current length of a line next to the cursor when the angle of the line is close to fixed values?

   A) Polar
   B) Snap
   C) Ortho
   D) Grid
   E) Fixed

6. You cannot have both Polar and Ortho active at the same time in AutoCAD.
   True/False

7. By turning a layer off you are deleting the objects on that layer from the drawing. True/False

8. Which of the following properties are not part of a layer definition?

   A) Color
   B) Snap
   C) Lineweight
   D) Linetype
   E) None of the above

9. What is the widest line used on an engineering drawing?

   A) Visible
   B) Hidden
   C) Cutting Plane
   D) Center
   E) Crosshatching

27

10. About how wide is that line?

   A) 0.01"
   B) 0.02"
   C) 0.03"
   D) 0.04"
   E) 0.05"

11. What are the two modes available for object snap called (pick 2)?

   A) Standard
   B) Running
   C) Selection
   D) Snapping
   E) Override

12. If a point you are trying to select is not on a snap point, OSNAP is useless. True/False

13. To activate a toolbar, you should right click on an existing toolbar and select the desired one from the list presented. True/False

Display Control

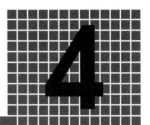

Objectives

1. Be able to ZOOM and PAN a drawing
2. Be able to use named views to display the correct portion of a drawing
3. Be able to change the visibility of a layer
4. Understand BLIPMODE
5. Refresh the display by using REDRAW or REGEN
6. Understand scaling of drawings
7. Use LTSCALE

Zoom and Pan

One of the advantages of a CAD system over traditional pencil and paper drawings is the ability to expand a portion of the drawing to make it easier to see what is being drawn. This feature is called zooming. AutoCAD has many options for the command ZOOM to allow you to display exactly the area of your drawing you desire. The keyboard command is ZOOM or just Z. The most common options are:

Window: The window option allows you to specify two points which form diagonally opposite corners of a rectangle. The portion of the drawing contained within that rectangle will be expanded to fill the screen, however, AutoCAD will not change the proportions of that which is displayed, it will show more of the drawing in one direction or another to keep it proportional. For instance, if the drawing on the left in Figure 4.1 were to have the ZOOM:Window performed, the result will be the drawing on the right.

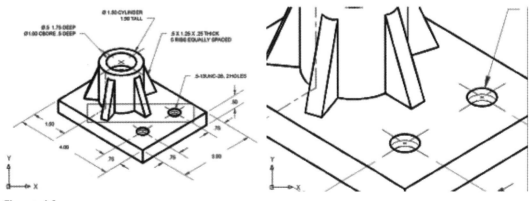

Figure 4.1

29

Extents: Once you have zoomed in, you may return to see the entire drawing by using the ZOOM:Extents option. This will fill the screen with everything you have drawn (and is on a thawed layer).

All: This option will fill the screen with all the objects you have drawn (like extents), but it will also insure that the entire Limits that are defined for the drawing are visible on screen.

Realtime: This will allow you to dynamically change the display of your drawing by zooming in (making it larger) or zooming out of the drawing by holding the left mouse button and moving the mouse up or down (side to side movement has no effect). By moving the mouse up, you cause the picture to get larger. The cursor will shift to a magnifying glass with a small + and – beside it.

Previous: AutoCAD stores the previous displays and will return to them, in sequence, by using ZOOM:Previous. AutoCAD will store 10 previous views.

Object: This will cause the display to scale itself so as to display the entirety of the selected objects. This may magnify the display or shrink it depending on the object(s) selected.

In addition to these options, if your system is equipped with an IntelliMouse or other mouse which has a roller wheel between the right and left buttons, you may roll the wheel to zoom in or out.

Unlike Zoom, PAN does not magnify the drawing, but allows you to slide the drawing under the monitor to display parts of the drawing which are currently off screen. Pan has no options; when you select the icon (or use PAN or just P through the keyboard) the cursor becomes a hand and by holding down the left mouse button, you can drag the contents of the window.

The IntelliMouse wheel can also be used to pan your drawing. By holding down on the wheel and moving the mouse you can drag the contents as with panning.

When using ZOOM:Previous to restore the previous view, changes via the PAN command count as views saved, so you can ZOOM:Previous to return to the view prior to panning the drawing. One limitation to using ZOOM:Previous is that the previous views are not saved with the drawing, so when you begin a new drawing session all previous zooms are lost.

Using Named Views

Sometimes you would like to be able to return to a particular zoomed area of the drawing without having to go through all the intermediate zooms you have performed. If you recognize that a display is important, you can save the Zoom/Pan information in a Named View. Using Named Views allows you to return to those saved displays directly, without having to zoom previous multiple times. To save a view you use the VIEW command or select the icon. This will display the view creation dialog box shown in Figure 4.2. Using this box you can create a New saved view. The New View dialog box will be displayed and you will be asked for a view name. If you have already zoomed in on the area of the drawing you want associated with the given

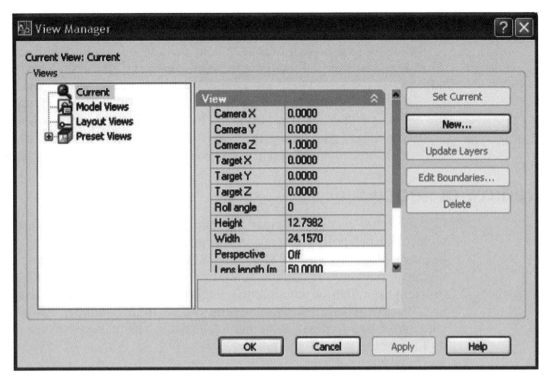

Figure 4.2

name, then all you need to do is select OK on the New View dialog box. This view name will now appear in the list of views below the view named Current.

Many of the items requested with this command are more suited to 3D drawings and we will come back and revisit the options later. For now, do not worry about the Preset Views tab as these are strictly 3D options.

If you have saved a view previously, you may restore it to the display by selecting the view from the list and selecting the Set Current button. Unlike Zoom:Previous, these display settings are saved with the drawing for future reference.

Controlling Layers

While zooming to display different parts of the drawing is important, another area of display control is working with layers. In the previous chapter, we talked about changing from one layer to another and why this could be useful for organizing your drawing. One of the other advantages of layers is the ability to independently control which layers of a drawing are displayed at any given time. You can sort of think of layers as drawings on sheets of clear plastic, which can be overlaid on each other.

To change the visibility of a layer, drop down the layer list (Figure 4.3) and click on the light bulb to the far left of the layer name. If the bulb is bright (yellow), then the objects on that layer will be displayed, if it is dark (gray) then they will not. In the example shown in Figure 4.3, the layers Border, Constr, and Window will not be displayed on the drawing. This is the equivalent of adding or removing one sheet of plastic from the stack of overlays.

Figure 4.3

Blips

One of the features of AutoCAD which can be enabled are Blips. Blips are simply small marks put on a drawing to indicate where the crosshairs were when the select button was pressed. These are temporary marks just placed on the display for the benefit of the drawer. If you do anything to redisplay the drawing on the screen, the old blips will disappear. This could be a Zoom, Pan or simply turning the grid off.

If you would like to see the Blips, use the command BLIPMODE. Simply turn BLIPMODE on and the blips will begin to appear, turn it off to stop them from appearing.

Redraw or Regen

One other method to clear the Blips from the screen is to force AutoCAD to recalculate the proper display of the drawing on the screen. The two commands to accomplish this are REDRAW and REGEN. The effect on the screen is virtually identical, but the calculations behind the two commands differ. On a very complex drawing the REDRAW command is slightly faster, but in some 3D applications it is less effective. The REDRAW command can be abbreviated by "R." For the beginning student the two commands are interchangeable. (Note: You can also remove the blips by turning the grid off and on.)

Scaling of Drawings

Many times a drawing will not fit on the paper at full scale, or it may appear too small. If this is the case, some basic changes need to be made to the operation of AutoCAD to allow these drawings to be completed. The information needed is simply the necessary scale to complete the drawing. This can be calculated by dividing the page size by the size of the object to be drawn (remember to account for multiple views and the space between them, if needed). Generally, the view spacing (and therefore, the space needed to dimension the views) is deducted from the page size along with the edge of the page margins, and this "effective page size" is divided by the sum of the object dimensions to arrive at a scale factor.

Once that scale is established, you have to shift your entire mind set from the method of drawing on paper to a new method for CAD. On paper you adjust the size of your object to fit on the page, in CAD you adjust the size of your page to fit the drawing. This is a necessity due to the first cardinal rule of Computer Drafting:

ALWAYS DRAW OBJECTS FULL SIZE IN THE COMPUTER

This allows different people to work on large projects and still share files without having to remember what scale everyone was working at.

Assuming that you are working from a basic template you should make the following changes BEFORE you begin your solution:

You must adjust the size of the border to account for the different page size. If you would have to reduce the size of the object to fit on the page, you must instead increase the size of the paper to accommodate the object. Thus if you were trying to draw a top view of a Boeing airplane which had to be scaled at 1 = 100, you would need to increase your border size by a factor of 100. This is done by using the SCALE command. You select the entire border and list the base point as 0,0. This will cause the border to stay in the upper right quadrant. The scale will be 100 in this case. After this scale the border will be well off screen, so you should do a zoom all to see the new border at its new size.

In order to get the grid to appear you will need to adjust the size of the grid by about the same factor. Since the default grid in the workbook templates is 0.2", you would need to change the grid to about 20". The command stream shown below uses a value of 24", thus having a 2 foot grid. However, when this is changed, the grid does not fill the border. Why?

The why deals with Limits. The grid will only fill the limits set for the drawing, and scaling the border does not reset the limits. This must be done with the LIMITS command. Both the lower left corner and the upper right corner values need to be multiplied by 100. Normally the lower left corner is the point (0,0), so multiplying it will still yield (0,0).

You will probably also need to adjust your snap to a convenient value based on what you are drawing and the precision needed there.

Other changes are in your mind set. If you want to leave 1" between the top and front views of the plane, then you will have to have a 100" gap in the computer, since everything will be reduced by a factor of 100 when it is eventually sent to hard copy. Likewise, your text height will have to be increased by a factor of 100 to be readable. (Think about taking your pencil out to the plane and printing in nice 1/8" single stroke gothic lettering the plane's serial number, then stepping back and taking a photo of the plane and printing that on a 8" x 10" picture. Do you think you could read what you wrote?)

The last change to discuss now (more changes will be necessary when we discuss dimensioning in Chapter 8) deals with dashed lines. Hidden and center lines will need to be adjusted just like the text height would. (Once again, go back to the concept of drawing a center line on the side of the plane and photographing it.) There is an overall scale factor that will adjust the size of all dashed lines in a drawing. It is called LTSCALE. By setting it to 100, all dashes and gaps in all dashed lines will be 100 times larger.

```
Command: scale
Select objects: 1 found
Select objects:
Specify base point:
Specify scale factor or [Copy/Reference] <1.0000>: 100
Command: zoom
Specify corner of window, enter a scale factor (nX or nXP), or
[All/Center/Dynamic/Extents/Previous/Scale/Window/Object] <real
     time>: _all
Command: grid
Specify grid spacing(X) or [ON/OFF/Snap/Major/aDaptive/Limits/
     Follow/Aspect]
<0.5000>: 24
Command: snap
Specify snap spacing or [ON/OFF/Aspect/Style/Type] <0.5000>: 12
Command: limits
Reset Model space limits:
Specify lower left corner or [ON/OFF] <0.0000,0.0000>:
Specify upper right corner <12.0000,9.0000>: 1000,750
Command: ltscale Enter new linetype scale factor <1.0000>: 100
Regenerating model.
```

Review Questions

1. Which of the following is not an option of the ZOOM command?

   A) Extents
   B) Limits
   C) All
   D) Previous
   E) Window

2. When you open a drawing you can use ZOOM:Previous to return to the previous display. True/False

3. By saving a view, you can return to view the exact area saved for that view. True/False

4. Temporary marks on the screen which mark where mouse clicks occurred are called

   A) plusses.
   B) crosses.
   C) blips.
   D) dots.
   E) markers.

5. If your grid does not fill your border, how might you fix that problem?

   A) Change grid settings
   B) Change snap settings
   C) Change limits settings
   D) Change zoom settings
   E) Change views

Paperspace, Modelspace, and Printing

Objectives

1. Be able to print a drawing
2. Understand the difference between Layout mode and Model mode

Printing Drawings

So far, we have learned the basics of creating drawings and it is time to discuss sending them to a printer. The full process of printing drawings in AutoCAD can be a bit intimidating, but once you see the rationale behind all the options and get some of the basic settings set up, the process can be streamlined greatly.

It all begins with the command PLOT (which comes from a time when pen plotters were the preferred method of drawing output). If you use the command PRINT, you will notice that it is aliased to the PLOT command. Doing this will launch the initial dialog box for printing shown in Figure 5.1.

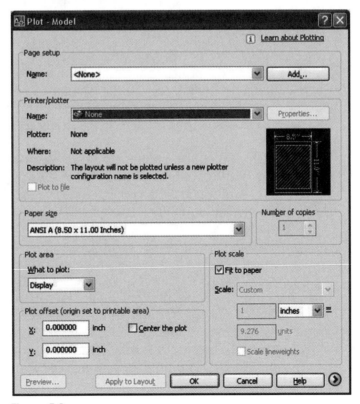

Figure 5.1

37

For most plotting applications, this is the only dialog box you will need. We will examine its options first to allow you to get output, then we will expand the dialog box and see what some of the more advanced options for plotting are.

There are several items which must be correctly set to give correct output. First, make sure the Plotter Name (here set to None and highlighted) is set to send your output to the desired printer. If your classroom is equipped with multiple printers this is very important and many a headache can be prevented by selecting the correct printer. The printer should be selected from the list of available printers on your computer.

Once you have selected your printer, you should check, in order:

Paper Size: This should be set to the correct size for your page (normally Letter).

Plot Area: Under the dropdown list for "What to Plot" your choices are: Limits (or Layout), Extents, Display, or Window. This is probably the second most misapplied section when plotting. You must know what it is you WANT to plot and then select the option that corresponds to your needs. Layout will plot all the drawing that falls on the theoretical page shown in the layout mode (this is discussed later during the section on 3D). It is only an option if you are in layout mode. If you are in model mode, then the option will be Limits and this will plot only that portion of your drawing which exists within the limits set for your drawing. Extents will plot your entire drawing, from top to bottom and left to right. Window will ask you to select diagonally opposite corners of a window and will plot the portion of the drawing that falls within this window. You can change the window by selecting the "WINDOW < " button (which will appear after you have selected your initial window) and picking diagonally opposite corners as you did initially.

Plot Scale: This determines the relationship between one unit in the drawing and one unit on the printed page. The printed page units are either inches or millimeters as determined by the dropdown selection made. This can make it awkward printing metric drawing in the U.S. (or American drawings outside America) since the printers are generally set to either ISO or Imperial paper sizes.

The scale is the most commonly misused setting when plotting. As a general rule, scaling your drawing to "Fit" is a *bad* option. It tells AutoCAD to calculate whatever scale factor is needed to get the Plot Area to fit on the Paper Size. You normally want to have to output printed at a specified scale. For a test print just to allow you to mark it up and make corrections this is not as important, but for work which is to be submitted it is critical. You can select a scale which prints your entire Plot Area on a small portion of the page, or you can select a scale which makes the Plot Area larger than the paper available. By looking at the small graphic of the sheet of paper in the Printer/plotter area of the dialog box you can see what area of the page will be occupied by the plot at the current settings. If the page has a red border, then the plot area is greater than the size of the page and some clipping will occur on the edges marked by red.

Plot Offset: This determines where on the page the lower left corner of the plot area will be located. The point 0,0 is the edge of the printable area, not the absolute corner of the page. Choosing the Center Plot option will place the center of the Plot Area at the center of the paper.

Once you have all the options set the way you think you want them, do a "Preview" (lower left corner of the dialog box) and see what is displayed as being the plotted output. AutoCAD will generate precisely what your output will look like on the printed page. The bottom line is: *If the print preview does not look right, the hard copy won't look right either!* Save a few trees and always do a Preview before sending the drawing to the printer.

Once your preview does look correct, select the small printer icon in the upper left corner of the preview screen to actually send the output to the printer. This will return you to your drawing. The only problem with this is that your plot settings are NOT saved to your file, and the next time you plot your drawing you will have to make all the corrections to the setting you just did. If you want to save your plot settings you must, before you send your output to the printer, select the "Apply to Layout" button on the plot dialog box. If you are in the preview mode, press ESC or select the small red X from the upper right corner to return to the plot dialog box. You can then apply your setting to the layout and then simply select OK to send your output to the printer. If you do not choose the Apply button, then the next time you plot this drawing you will have to reset all these settings. Apply stores the plot setting with the file for the next and all future plots.

These five settings: Plotter Name, Paper Size, Plot Area, Plot Offset and Plot Scale are the ones most commonly modified from plot to plot. There are several additional parameters which should be checked initially and may need to be changed under special conditions. These are accessed by expanding the dialog box via the arrow (actually it is a > sign) in the lower right corner of the basic box. Selecting this will expand the dialog into the one shown in Figure 5.2.

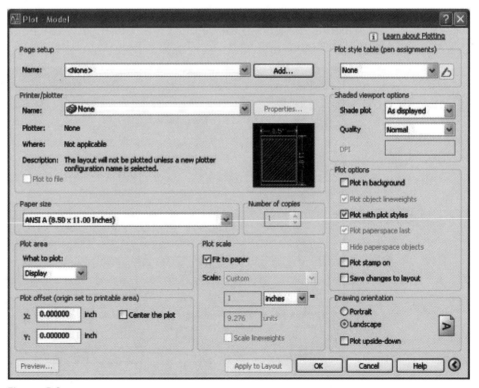

Figure 5.2

The Plot Style Table is used to control how the printer handles colors. If you leave the setting to None, then the printer will decide how it interprets color data, either by printing it in full color, dithering it to a gray scale, or printing in black and white. Leaving a decision up to a piece of hardware is generally a bad idea, and you would like to have more control over the process since there is more which can be done with a plot style table than simply controlling color.

You can set your plot styles to print each AutoCAD color with a particular line weight, thus overriding the layer settings. This is generally not recommended. The proper place to set line weights is on the layer, since that determines the functionality of the object. In order to adjust the line weights in this manner you must edit the Plot Style Table.

Since engineering drawings are normally presented in black and white the logical plot style table is named "monochrome" and can be found in the dropdown list. It is possible that your instructor has created a plot style table precisely for this course. If so make sure you use that style. The information contained in a plot style includes color mapping and line weight specifications, so the correct style table will make your visible lines bold and your hidden lines thinner. If all your lines are printing very thin, then you need to check the setting for the plot style table. Likewise, if your lines are varying in the shades of gray, check your style table setting. Normally this need only be done once per drawing, since the settings stay with the drawing, not the computer. The template file can even have this information embedded in it.

Until you begin drawing in 3D, the Shaded viewport options are irrelevant.

Plot Options: You normally want to "Plot with Plot Styles" since this is a good way to control the appearance of your output. Plotting paperspace last does not really make any difference for printers, however if you are using a pen plotter it is good to print all of the drawing first and the border last. If you are printing a drawing which does not have a border or a place for you to put your name and identification information you can turn on the Plot Stamp and select what information you want AutoCAD to print. By selecting the icon to the right of the option you activate the dialog box shown in Figure 5.3.

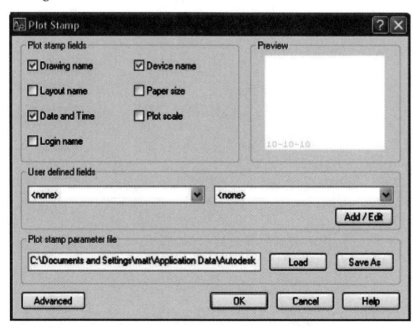

Figure 5.3

The final option under plot options is "Save changes to layout." If you select this option, when your plot is sent to the printer, your options are automatically saved for the next plot, thus eliminating the need to select the "Apply to Layout" button on the dialog box. Since, in a classroom setting, the parameters are normally set once and do not change for a specific drawing, it is good to select this option.

Drawing Orientation: Either Portrait or Landscape depending on the setup of your drawing.

Using Layout Mode

Many first year courses do not plot the 2D drawings using Layout Mode. If your drawing on the Model Tab has a border and title information, then you do not need to use Layout mode until you begin constructing drawings in 3D.

To facilitate laying out of drawings for printing, AutoCAD uses a special system called LAYOUT mode. When you create a new drawing from scratch, you will be able to see that there are three tabs near the lower left side of the drawing labeled Model, Layout1, and Layout2. When you select one of the layout modes for the first time, you will be presented with a dialog box asking about the configuration of the page you want to use for this layout. This box is very similar to the plotting dialog box and the parameters should be set as in the plot dialog boxes above. What will then be displayed is a special area of the drawing called Paperspace, while your drawing is done in Modelspace.

One reason for mentioning it here is the inevitable chance that you clicked the button at the bottom of the screen labeled "Model" and you were taken directly to Layout mode and Paper Space (as indicated by the background changing from black to white). Unfortunately, just clicking on the button (now labeled Paper) will not get you back to where you were. If this happens, all you have to do is select the tab labeled Model and you will be restored to normal model space and drawing mode.

It is also possible to create a layout which includes border information and then to display your model in the layout view by creating a viewport through which the model can be seen. This is a little more advanced concept and will only be mentioned in passing here, but by using the Zoom command the model can be scaled so that you can use the same border without modifications to plot any scale model necessary.

Editing, The True Power of CAD

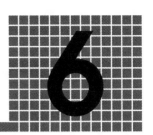

Objectives

1. Be able to create selection sets in AutoCAD
2. To be able to edit your drawings in AutoCAD
3. The ability to use keyboard coordinates
4. To be able to use Grips to edit drawings in real time
5. To be able to change the layer of an object already created
6. Edit already created text
7. Modify the basic properties of an object
8. Create or modify a text style

By now, you have the ability to create some fairly complex drawings in AutoCAD. You can draw lines, circles, arcs, and write text. You can plot your drawings and get high quality output from the computer. All these things are good, however they are just the tip of the iceberg of CAD. Using the tools currently at your disposal, you will not be much more productive than using traditional hand methods. This chapter will open the doors to increasing your productivity and making CAD pay for itself.

As the chapter title says, the true power of CAD does not lie in the creating of lines, but in the ability to edit them. It lies in the ability to draw something once and never have to create that part again, to be able to copy that part to wherever it is needed. It lies in the ability to create construction lines which can be perfectly erased. It lies in the ability to *edit* a drawing.

Selection Sets

We have actually already used one editing command, ERASE. Using that command we can begin to see the applications of selection sets. Selection sets are the beginning of any editing command. They determine what objects are to be edited. For the ERASE command they determine what objects will be deleted from the drawing and which will remain. In all editing commands there is a need to specify precisely which objects will be the target of the edit and this is what selection sets do.

A selection set is formed in response to the prompt "Select Objects:" in AutoCAD. From this prompt you will select the objects you want to be the target of the editing command. You do not have to simply select the objects one at a time (although this is an option), there are many options available for selecting the objects in groups. The simplest two are Windowing and Crossing as described earlier. Three additional options which do not require using the mouse are:

Last: this selects the last object drawn in the drawing

Previous: this re-selects the last selection set operated on

All: this selects all the objects in the drawing, regardless of layer

Using those six options for selection sets will allow you to make use of the full editing capabilities of AutoCAD.

The editing commands available on the Modify toolbar are shown in Figure 6.1.

Move and Copy

The MOVE and COPY commands function exactly the same, except the COPY command leaves a copy of the selected objects behind. They begin like all the other editing commands by requesting what you want to move or copy. You must form a selection set containing the objects you want and then press enter to terminate the selection set process.

You will be asked for two points, specifying a displacement vector over which the objects will be translated. Once you select the second point, the command will be executed and you will be returned to the Command: prompt.

	Erase
	Copy
	Mirror
	Offset
	Array
	Move
	Rotate
	Scale
	Stretch
	Trim
	Extend
	Break (at a point)
	Break
	Join
	Chamfer
	Fillet
	Explode

Figure 6.1

```
Command: copy

Select objects: {pick those objects you want to move}
Specify opposite corner: 33 found

Select objects: {press Enter when you have completed your
      selections}
Specify base point or displacement, or [Multiple]: {pick the
      beginning point for the copy vector}
Specify second point of displacement or <use first point as
      displacement>: {drag the copies to the correct location}
```

Break, Trim, and Extend

These three commands form a loosely related set. Break and Trim allow you to remove a portion of an object without erasing the entire object and Extend is the inverse operation for Trim.

To break an object, simply select the object at one side of the break and select the other end of the break for the second point. The "break at a point" icon simply uses the selected point as both the first and last point, thus splitting a line or arc into two distinct pieces.

```
Command: break
Select object:
Specify second break point or [First point]:
```

The trim command will remove a portion of an object like the break command, but it requires the existence of objects to form a boundary for the trimming operation. If you wanted to remove the portion of the line which is inside the circle as shown in Figure 6.2, you would have the circle be your cutting edge and the central portion of the line as the object for trim.

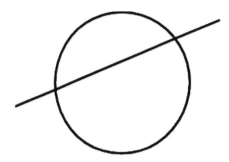

Figure 6.2

```
Command: trim
Current settings: Projection=UCS,
     Edge=None
Select cutting edges ...
Select objects: {pick circle} 1 found

Select objects:
Select object to trim or shift-select to extend or [Project/
     Edge/Undo]: {pick center of line}
Select object to trim or shift-select to extend or [Project/
     Edge/Undo]:
```

If you do not choose any cutting edges (i.e. just press enter at that prompt), then AutoCAD will act as if you had selected the entire drawing as cutting edges, thus any item to trim will be trimmed to the nearest intersection.

The extend command works just backward from the trim command. You must still specify boundaries, but these are the boundaries to which the objects will be extended.

Notice that you can extend objects using the TRIM command by holding the shift key when selecting the object to extend.

Chamfer and Fillet

Both these commands join existing lines or arcs. The fillet command will lay in a radius to complete the intersection while the Chamfer will extend the objects until they intersect and then cut a sharp corner from that intersection. In each case, the lines or arcs will be extended or trimmed as needed to reach the point of intersection prior to filleting or chamfering.

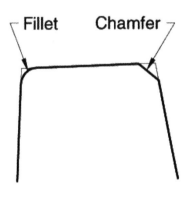

Figure 6.3

```
Command: fillet

Current settings: Mode = TRIM, Radius =
     0.2500
Select first object or [Polyline/
     Radius/Trim]: R
Specify fillet radius <0.2500>: .5

Select first object or [Polyline/Radius/Trim]:
Select second object:
```

```
Command: chamfer

(TRIM mode) Current chamfer Dist1 = 0.5000, Dist2 = 0.5000
Select first line or [Polyline/Distance/Angle/Trim/Method]: T

Enter Trim mode option [Trim/No trim] <Trim>:

Select first line or [Polyline/Distance/Angle/Trim/Method]: M

Enter trim method [Distance/Angle] <Distance>:

Select first line or [Polyline/Distance/Angle/Trim/Method]:
Select second line:
```

Notice that you must specifically alter the fillet radius (or chamfer distances) prior to selecting the objects to be filleted. The Trim option will allow you to not have the objects extended to their intersection before applying a fillet or chamfer.

By default the commands will apply one fillet or chamfer and will then terminate. By using the multiple option, the command will stay active until you cancel it.

Zero Radius Fillets: A Useful Trick

One useful method which combines the functionality of TRIM, EXTEND, and FILLET into one operation is to set the radius for a fillet to zero and set the trim mode to TRIM. Then apply a fillet to any two non-parallel lines or arcs and the objects will be extended/trimmed to a sharp corner.

Other Editing Commands

Mirror

The mirror command will create a mirror image of the selected objects. You must select the objects to be mirrored and then select two points to define the line about which they will be mirrored. You can choose to retain or delete the original objects.

```
Command: mirror
Select objects: Specify opposite corner: 14 found

Select objects:
Specify first point of mirror line:
Specify second point of mirror line:
Delete source objects? [Yes/No] <N>:
```

Offset

Offset will create a copy of an object in a parallel fashion. For lines it will create a parallel line, for arcs or circles it will create a concentric arc or circle. You may either specify the distance between the objects or a point through which the offset copy must pass.

```
Command: offset
Specify offset distance or [Through] <1.0000>: .50

Select object to offset or <exit>:
Specify point on side to offset:
Select object to offset or <exit>:
```

Scale

Scale will allow you to increase or decrease the physical size of objects in your selection set. You must specify a base point about which all the scaling will occur.

```
Command: scale
Select objects: Specify opposite corner: 15 found
Select objects:
Specify base point:
Specify scale factor or [Reference]: .5
```

Stretch

Stretch will allow you to move one end of a line or arc without moving the other. The resulting object will be longer or shorter than the original. The prompts are essentially the same as for the move command.

```
Command: stretch
Select objects to stretch by crossing-window or crossing-
        polygon...
Select objects: Specify opposite corner: 2 found

Select objects:
Specify base point or displacement:
Specify second point of displacement or <use first point as
        displacement>:
```

It is worth observing the statement that selections must be made with a crossing window or crossing polygon. For this command you cannot just select an object and go, you must use a crossing selection and thereby specify not only the object, but which end of it you want to move.

Lengthen

Lengthen will modify the length of a line or arc. You can change the total length, the amount to be added (or subtracted), a percentage change, or, for arcs, the included angle can be modified.

```
Command: lengthen

Select an object or [DElta/Percent/Total/DYnamic]:
Current length: 2.0507
Select an object or [DElta/Percent/Total/DYnamic]: T
Specify total length or [Angle] <1.0000)>: 2.25

Select an object to change or [Undo]:
Select an object to change or [Undo]:
```

Join

Join will take to collinear line segments, coradial arcs, of contigious polylines and form one object from them. It can also be used to convert an arc to a full circle, in essence closing it to itself.

```
Command: join
Select source object:
Select lines to join to source: 1 found
Select lines to join to source:
1 line joined to source
```

Array

Array is used to make many copies of a set of objects in a regular pattern, either rectangular or circular. A rectangular array makes copies of objects in rows and columns, similar to the arrangement of the desks in a classroom or windows on a high-rise building. A circular (actually called polar by AutoCAD) makes copies equally spaced along an arc or circle, like the spokes on a wheel or teeth on a gear.

For a rectangular array you must specify the number of columns and the number of rows. Columns are vertical lines offset in the "X" direction, rows are horizontal lines offset in the "Y" direction. Once you have specified how many columns and rows you want, you must specify the offset in both "X" and "Y." This is the distance from one point on the objects to the identical point on the next copy. Figure 6.4 shows an array of 3 rows and 5 columns of a diameter 1 circle, with row and column spacing of 0.75 in both directions.

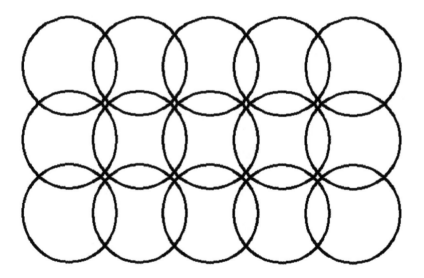

Figure 6.4

To create this pattern draw a diameter 1.00" circle and then use the array command. It will display the following dialog box (Figure 6.5). Complete the box as shown and select the circle under the "Select objects" button.

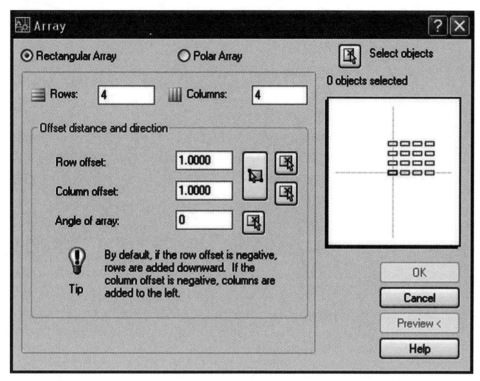

Figure 6.5

A polar array requires you to specify a center point, the total angle to be filled, and the number of items (or angle between items). The dialog box looks like Figure 6.6.

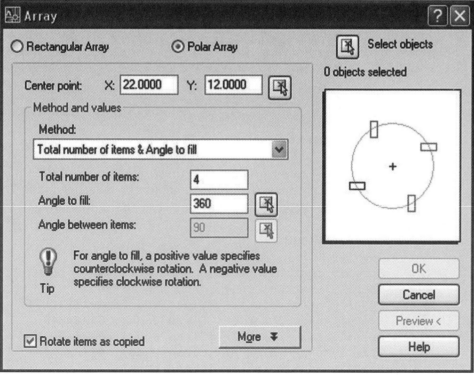

Figure 6.6

And, if completed as shown above, with the two lines selected, will convert the figure on the left into the one on the right as shown in Figure 6.7.

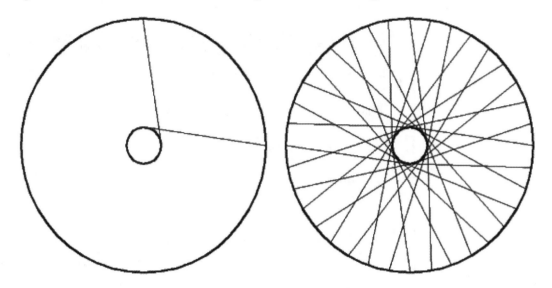

Figure 6.7

One particularly useful application of the array command is to draw threads on a bolt or inside a nut. This application combines keyboard coordinates and array to generate detailed threads on a bolt.

Problem: Draw detailed threads for the 1.5-6UNC-2A bolt shown in Figure 6.8. The length of engagement is 3.25".

Figure 6.8

The process we will follow is to draw one portion of the thread and then array it with one row and many columns to create the thread symbol. To begin the drawing we start a new drawing and draw one copy of the first thread.

```
Command: LINE
Specify first point:
Specify next point or [Undo]: @1/6<60
Specify next point or [Undo]: @1/6<-60
Specify next point or [Close/Undo]: @-1/12,1.5
Specify next point or [Close/Undo]: @1/6<240
Specify next point or [Close/Undo]: @1/6<0
Specify next point or [Close/Undo]: @1/6<120
Specify next point or [Close/Undo]:
```

Before going any further, it is important to understand what the keyboard coordinates used above actually did, and why. The first two sets drew the lower "V." Since we know the thread has 6 threads per inch (from the 6UNC portion of the note) we know the pitch is 1/6 of an inch and a UNC thread has a 60° thread angle. This means that the sides of the "V" make an equilateral triangle, with each side being 1/6". The next entry "@1/12,1.5" is probably the most confusing one. It draws the crest line on the thread, going backward in the "X" direction one half of a thread (1/12, not 1/6) and up the major diameter of the thread (from the 1.5 portion of the thread note). It is a relative Cartesian format. The next three entries draw the triangle at the top.

Having completed this your drawings should look like Figure 6.9. There is one extra line, the horizontal one, which we drew for construction. It should now be erased.

Figure 6.9

```
Command: erase
Select objects: {select short horizontal line} 1
      found
Select objects:
```

We now have to add the root line, which must be added using OSNAP to find the exact root points on the "V"'s of the thread.

```
Command: LINE
Specify first point: endp of
Specify next point or [Undo]: endp of
Specify next point or [Undo]:
```

This should result in Figure 6.10, which is one copy of the thread. It now needs to be arrayed along the length of the bolt. You must first figure out how many copies of the objects you will need. Since the length of engagement is 3.5", and each thread is 1/6" long, you will need 3.5*6 copies, or 21 copies of the objects as columns, and one row with a column spacing of 1/6". Use the array command and complete the dialog box as shown in Figure 6.11.

Figure 6.10

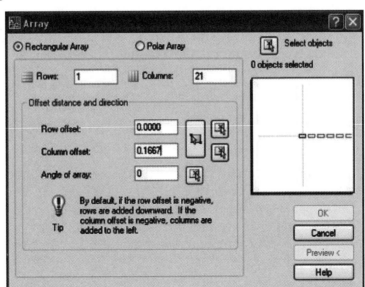

Figure 6.11

You should get the following results (Figure 6.12):

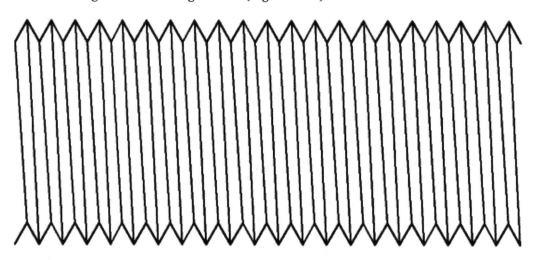

Figure 6.12

All that has to be done now is to complete the end of the bolt with a chamfer, then add whatever head type is desired.

Additional Selection Options

Three more options exist for the creation of selection sets in AutoCAD. They are a little more specialized, but add great flexibility to select the necessary objects. They are:

WP (Window Polygon)—Window polygon allows you to draw an irregular polygon by selecting points at its vertices. Any object which lies complete within the resulting polygon will be selected. It is analogous to the Window option described earlier.

CP (Crossing Polygon)—This combines the features of a crossing with the features of a polygon. Thus you can select points at the vertices of a polygon and select everything within or touching the resulting polygon.

Fence—The fence option works like CP, but it does not form a closed polygon, simply a path. Anything which touches this path will be selected; however it is not capable of surrounding anything.

Remember that objects can be removed from the selection set by holding down the shift key and selecting the objects individually.

Grips

In addition to the commands discussed above, AutoCAD has another method to allow you to make changes on the objects in your drawing. Grips can be used to accomplish some of the more common editing tasks. These include: Move, Copy, Stretch, Rotate, Scale, and Mirror as well as giving you the ability to move an object from one layer to another. To activate the grips on an object, you must left click on an object while there is no active command (i.e. the command prompt is "Command:"). This will highlight the object and display small blue squares on it. These blue squares are the grips and they mark the points available for editing. The number and location of the squares is dependent on the object. Figure 6.13 shows the grip locations for the objects we have seen so far.

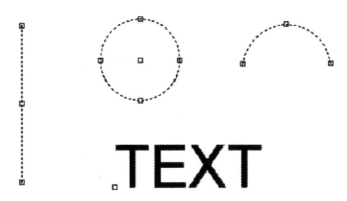

Figure 6.13

The blue grips are called "cold grips" and are just markers. To activate a grip and make it a "hot grip" click on that grip and it will turn red and be filled in and the command line will offer you the chance to stretch that grip to a new location. By pressing the enter key you can cycle through the five editing options, or you can right click and select them directly from the popup menu shown in Figure 6.14.

Once you activate grips on an object, the layer box will show whatever layer that object is drawn on (if you activate more than one object and they are on different layers, the box will go blank). To change that object to a new layer, just drop down the list of layers and select the new layer.

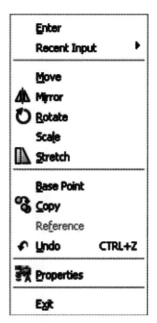

Figure 6.14

When you have finished making your modifications with grips, you can clear them by pressing escape on the keyboard two times (the first time will unhighlight the object without clearing the grips). If you invoke an editing command while the objects are still highlighted with grips, then the highlighted objects will become the selection set used for that editing command and no further selection prompt will be made. This can be very helpful at times, but you can get into trouble if you inadvertently forget to cancel grips and then use the ERASE command. If this happens, don't panic, just remember the Undo command and you can recover from your mistake.

Editing of Text

Text can be edited by using the command DDEDIT. This will request that you select a text string. The contents of that selection will be displayed in an edit text dialog box (Figure 6.15) and you can make whatever changes necessary. This is a common method when filling out title blocks. Rather than recreating each text entry from scratch, simply edit the existing text to add your name.

Figure 6.15

One other text operation available in AutoCAD is basic spell checking. The SPELL command will check a selection for spelling errors and display the proposed changes.

Object Properties

Each object created has certain properties associated with it. Many of these can be modified directly by using the command PROPERTIES. This command will activate a dialog box of sorts. It can be moved and docked at the side of the screen and will contain properties for editing, depending on what object(s) are selected using grips. Figure 6.16 shows four different object types: Line, Circle, Arc, and Text and the properties available for each.

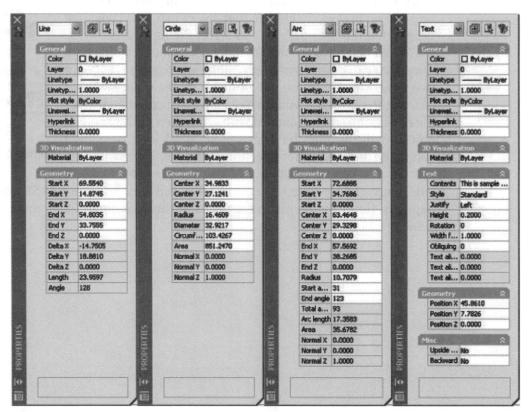

Figure 6.16

Review Questions

1. When forming a selection set, the LAST option will select the last object drawn. True/False

2. Using the BREAK command on a circle will yield 2 arcs. True/False

3. When TRIMMING an object, you must first select the object, then where you want to trim it. True/False

4. You can extend objects when using the TRIM command. True/False

5. When creating an offset from an arc, which of the following is true?

    A) The new arc will have the same radius as the existing arc.
    B) The new arc will have the same center point as the existing one.
    C) The new arc will be larger than the existing arc.
    D) The new arc will be smaller than the existing arc.
    E) None of the above.

6. If you drew a unit square (i.e. one unit on a side) and used the array command to make 3 rows and 3 columns, what spacings would you use to get the picture shown to the right?

    A) Row = 0, Column = 1
    B) Row = 1, Column = 0
    C) Row = 0, Column = 2
    D) Row = 2, Column = 1
    E) Row = 1, Column = 2

7. You can use the stretch command to convert a circle into an ellipse. True/False

8. You can use grips to draw a circle into an elliptical shape. True/False

9. Which of the following is not an option when editing objects with grips?

    A) ARRAY
    B) MOVE
    C) ROTATE
    D) STRETCH
    E) MIRROR

10. AutoCAD includes a command to spell check the text in your drawing. True/False

11. When using a polygon to form a selection set

    A) if it is drawn counter-clockwise it will default to a crossing polygon.
    B) it will automatically close using a straight segment when you press enter.
    C) it has a maximum of 10 vertices.
    D) the polygon must be an existing object in AutoCAD which is selected to enclose other objects.
    E) AutoCAD does not support a polygon option for forming selection sets.

55

12. A zero radius fillet will form a sharp corner between two non-parallel lines. True/False

13. The previous option will not work for forming selection sets if the previous editing command was ERASE. True/False

Pictorials

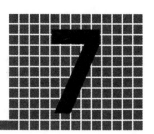

Objectives

1. Be able to create Oblique drawings in AutoCAD
2. Be able to set GRID and SNAP to allow drawing in isometric mode
3. The ability to use keyboard coordinates
4. Be able to draw isometric ellipses in AutoCAD
5. Be able to apply pseudo-isometric fillets using the FILLET command

Keyboard Coordinates

In addition to using the mouse to specify points in AutoCAD, it is possible to type a location in directly via the keyboard. This is called using keyboard coordinates. There are two formats of keyboard coordinates: Absolute or Relative. An absolute coordinate references the origin of the drawing, while a relative one references the last point selected. Absolute is the default; to note a relative coordinate place an "@" before the coordinate values.

There are also two styles of keyboard coordinates: Cartesian and polar. Cartesian coordinates reference X and Y, while polar reference a distance and an angle from the horizontal. For Cartesian, the format is simply "X,Y" and for polar it is "dist < angle."

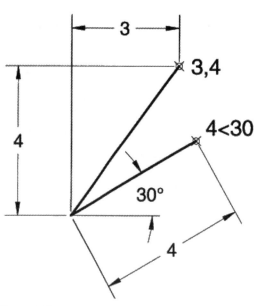

Figure 7.1

You can mix either format with either style to allow for four different input formats. These are:

Absolute Cartesian: 3,4
Relative Cartesian: @3,4
Absolute Polar: 4 < 30
Relative Polar: @4 < 30

Another option for specifying a point via the keyboard is the Direct Distance option. If AutoCAD is requesting a point, you may type a single number in through the keyboard. AutoCAD will measure the angle from the last point selected to the current locations of the crosshairs and will select a point as if these were the result of a relative polar input using the specified distance in the direction of the crosshairs.

Using keyboard coordinates along with the copy command is a good way to generate oblique pictorial drawings.

Example:

Draw a Cavalier Oblique of the object shown in Figure 7.2.

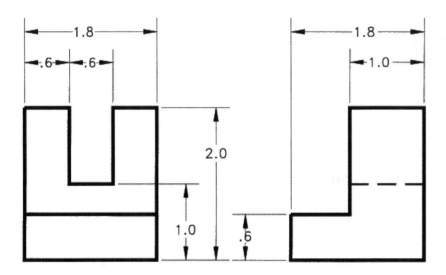

Figure 7.2

1. Draw the front view using normal AutoCAD commands and techniques.

2. Use the COPY command to replicate the front view to depict the depth.

```
Command: COPY
Select objects: Other corner: 11 found
Select objects:
<Base point or displacement>/Multiple: m
Base point:
Second point of displacement: @.8<40
Second point of displacement: @1.8<40
Second point of displacement:
```

3. ERASE the portions of the depth profiles which will not be seen.

```
Command: erase
Select objects:
Select objects:
...
Select objects:
Select objects:
```

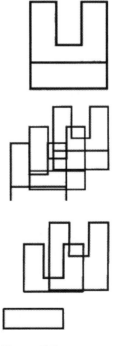

Figure 7.3

4. Add receding lines using OSNAP and the LINE command.

```
Command: line
From Point: endp of
To Point: endp of
To Point:
...
```

5. TRIM and ERASE the remaining lines which would not be visible.

```
Command: TRIM
Select cutting edges: (Projmode = UCS, Edgemode = No extend)
Select objects: 1 found
Select objects:
<Select object to Trim>/Project/Edge/Undo:
<Select object to trim>/Project/Edge/Undo:
```

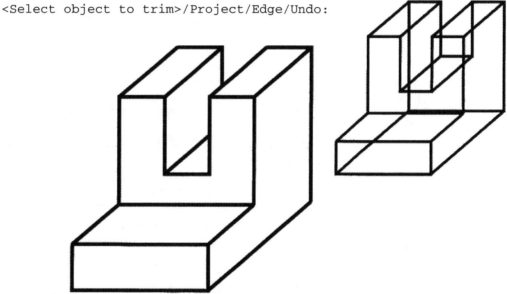

Figure 7.4

Using Isometric Mode

Unlike drawing Obliques, AutoCAD has a special mode to assist in the construction of Isometric drawings. By changing the SNAP to isometric mode, the crosshairs will re-orient themselves to follow the isometric axes. An example is shown in Figure 7.5.

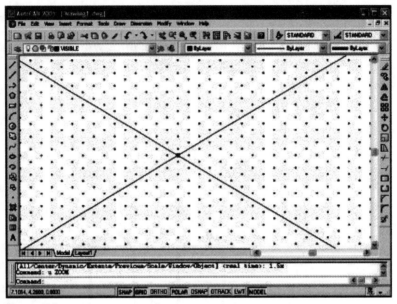

Figure 7.5

Looking at the figure, you will also notice that the grid has shifted from the regular orthographic grid you have been familiar with to an isometric grid. The crosshairs can be flipped from the orientation shown to drawing on a left (front) or a right isometric plane by pressing function key F5. An example of each of these is shown in Figures 7.6 and 7.7.

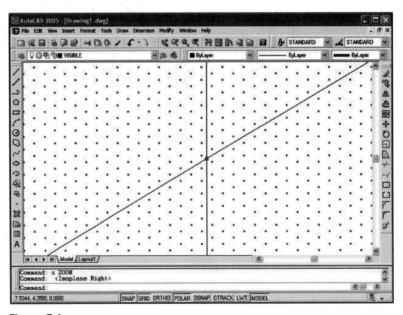

Figure 7.6

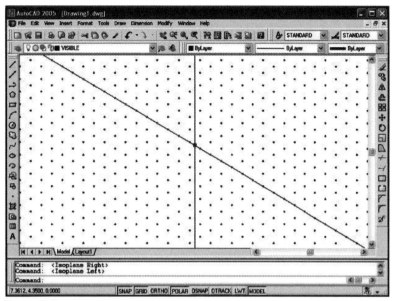

Figure 7.7

Once you are in this mode, isometric drawings can be done as easily as any other drawing. Simply draw lines as needed. The mode ORTHO will restrict the crosshairs to following the crosshairs, so whichever isometric plane the crosshairs are orientated with, the lines you draw will be parallel to those isometric axes. You can also use the same method used for drawing obliques: draw one view, use copy to make the back side, connect with lines.

The one big question which has not been answered yet is, "How do I get into isometric mode?" To activate this mode, you must adjust SNAP by changing its settings. Right click on the snap button on the status line and choose settings. You will be presented with the dialog box shown in Figure 7.8. In the lower right corner of the box you can select the Snap type and style. You want to use Grid snap and Isometric snap as is illustrated in the figure. This will activate the isometric crosshairs. To return to orthographic snap repeat the process and choose Rectangular snap.

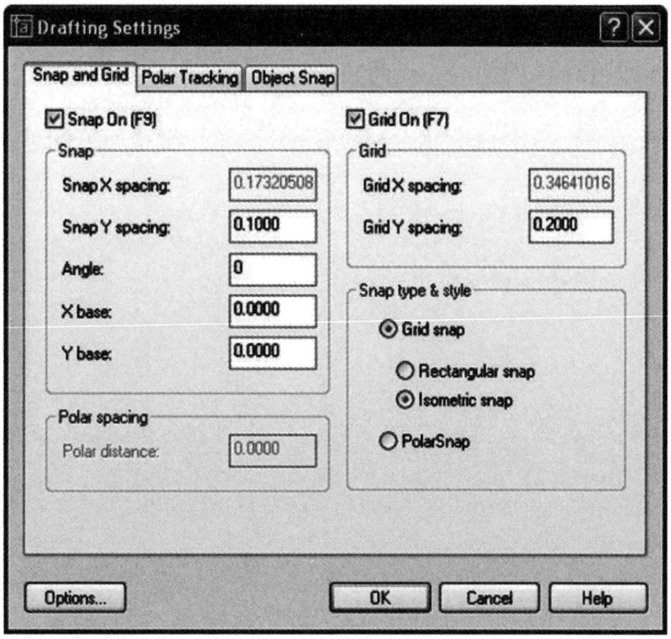

Figure 7.8

As long as your drawing is composed of only straight lines you are ready to draw. However, if you have circular features in your object, then they will appear as ellipses in an isometric drawing. As long as they lie parallel to one of the isometric planes they can easily be drawn with the ELLIPSE command. For many objects this is the case.

Using the ELLIPSE command for isometric drawings can be a little tricky, since that command is designed to be flexible and allow ellipses of any shape or size to be drawn. Isometric ellipses have a particular aspect ratio (the ratio of minor diameter to major diameter). To force AutoCAD to draw ellipses of the particular aspect ratio for isometrics you must use an option within the ellipse command called "ISOCIRCLE." This is only valid if the snap is set to isometric mode. The trick is that the option must be chosen before you select any points to define the ellipse. The command line stream below shows the construction of an isometric ellipse and the resulting figure (Figure 7.9) is shown as well.

```
Command: ellipse
Specify axis endpoint of
        ellipse or [Arc/
        Center/Isocircle]:
        isocircle
Specify center of
        isocircle: {select with
        mouse}
Specify radius of isocircle
        or [Diameter]: 0.25
```

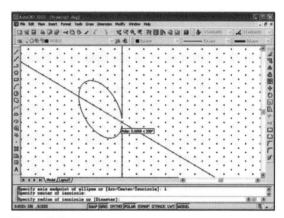

Figure 7.9

Notice that the ellipse is oriented on the same plane as the isometric crosshairs are. If you wanted an ellipse oriented on the top plane, just change your crosshairs to that orientation prior to completing the ellipse command.

Ellipses behave as circles do for the most part. They can be snapped to using OSNAP:Center, Quadrant, or Tangent, however they will not accept a deferred tangent osnap (where you select tangent to the ellipse first and then select the end of the line). They break and trim like circles.

You can use that last fact when you need to draw a portion of an ellipse (elliptical arc), like the top of a tombstone. Draw the entire ellipse, and then trim or break the ellipse to remove the unwanted portion. The command stream below shows the construction of a tombstone shape. Notice that there is a problem in drawing the tangent line between the two ellipses (since one has to be a deferred tangent) and the problem is resolved by using the OSNAP mode Nearest and "eyeballing" the initial tangent.

```
Command: LINE
Specify first point:
Specify next point or
        [Undo]:
Specify next point or
        [Undo]:
Specify next point or
        [Close/Undo]:
Specify next point or
        [Close/Undo]:
```

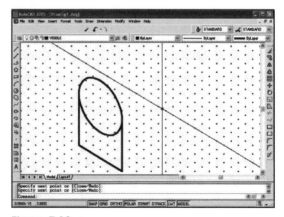

Figure 7.10

```
Command: ellipse
Specify axis endpoint of ellipse or [Arc/Center/Isocircle]: i
Specify center of isocircle:
Specify radius of isocircle or [Diameter]:
Command: copy
Select objects: 1 found
Select objects: 1 found, 2
      total
Select objects: 1 found, 3
      total
Select objects: 1 found, 4
      total
Select objects:
Specify base point or
      displacement, or
      [Multiple]:
Specify second point of
      displacement or <use
      first point as
      displacement>:
```

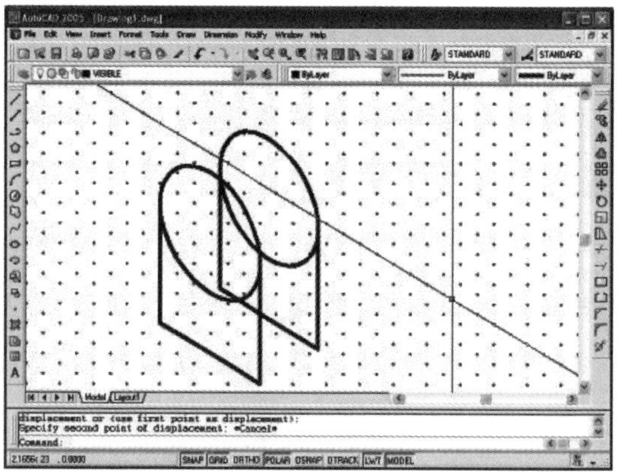

Figure 7.11

```
Command: LINE
Specify first point: <Isoplane Top>{press F5 to which planes}
Specify next point or [Undo]:
Specify next point or [Undo]:
Command:LINE
Specify first point: nea to
      <Snap off>
Specify next point or [Undo]:
      tan to
Specify next point or [Undo]:
Command: ERASE
Select objects: 1 found
Select objects: 1 found, 2
      total
Select objects:
Command: trim
Current settings:
      Projection=UCS,
      Edge=None
```

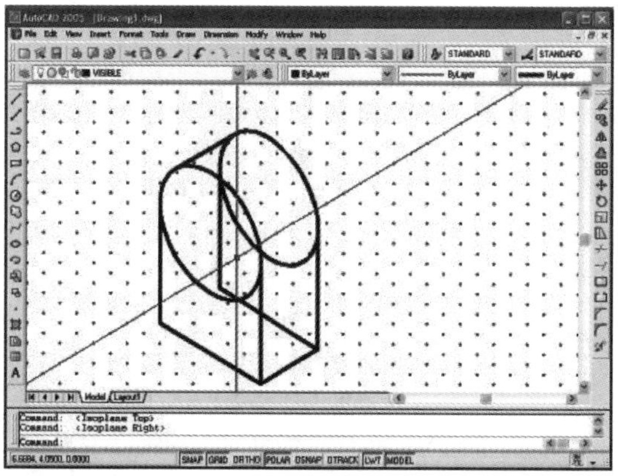

Figure 7.12

```
Select cutting edges ...
Select objects: {select tangent line} 1 found
Select objects: {select rear vertical line} 1 found, 2 total
Select objects:
Select object to trim or
      shift-select to extend
      or [Project/Edge/
      Undo]:
Select object to trim or
      shift-select to extend
      or [Project/Edge/
      Undo]:
Command: TRIM
Current settings:
      Projection=UCS,
      Edge=None
```

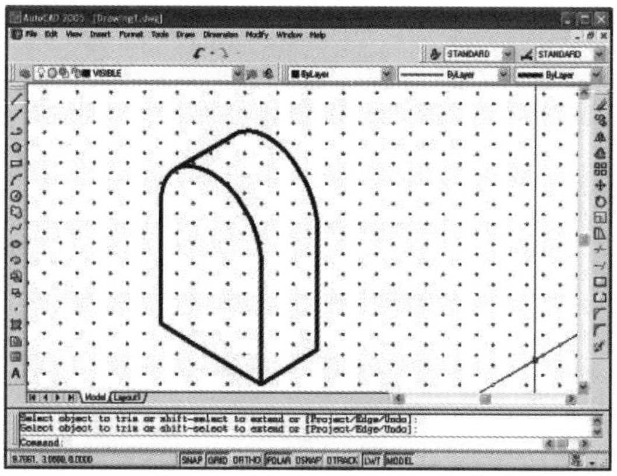

Figure 7.13

```
Select cutting edges ...
Select objects: 1 found
Select objects: 1 found, 2 total
Select objects:
Select object to trim or shift-select to extend or [Project/
     Edge/Undo]:
Select object to trim or shift-select to extend or [Project/
     Edge/Undo]:
```

Isometric Fillets

One final item needs to be addressed with regard to isometrics: the use of the FILLET command. One of the fastest ways to *ruin* an isometric drawing is to use the fillet command in AutoCAD to apply isometric fillets. The fillet command draws circular arcs, NOT isometric arcs. As such, it is not appropriate to use. Figure 7.14 shows an ellipse of radius 1 and a fillet of radius 1 on the circumscribing rhombus. Note that there is a substantial difference.

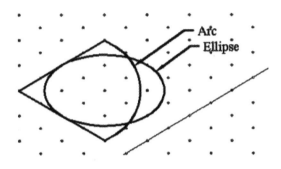

Figure 7.14

However, it is possible to use the fillet command if one is sneaky and remembers an old method used to construct ellipses by hand called the four center method. In short, the four center method replaces a true ellipse with four arcs of differing radii and different centers to approximate the shape of an ellipse. It is reasonably accurate and for small arcs is quite sufficient. Figure 7.15 shows the four center ellipse corresponding to the radius 1 ellipse (shown as a dashed feature in the figure). The numbers 1.7321 and 0.5774 correspond to the square root of 3 and 1 over the square root of 3, respectively. Thus, if you modify the radius used for the fillet command by a factor of the square root of 3, you can approximate an elliptical fillet with a circular one. This only works for 90 degree fillets between lines parallel to the isometric axes.

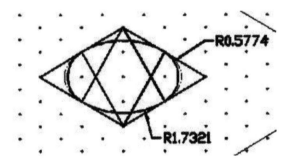

Figure 7.15

Review Questions

1. In order to draw a line 3 units long at an angle of 40 degrees from the X axis, what would be the correct response to the "To point:" prompt?

   A) 3,40
   B) 3 < 40
   C) @3,40
   D) @3 < 40
   E) 40 > 3

2. When drawing lines in AutoCAD, if you type in "5" and press return in response to a "To point:" prompt, AutoCAD will

   A) issue an error message.
   B) request a "Y" value and then draw the line segment.
   C) draw a line 5 units long.
   D) request an angle and draw a line 5 units at the specified angle.
   E) none of the above.

3. In order to access the isometric mode in AutoCAD, you must adjust the settings of

   A) GRID.
   B) LIMITS.
   C) ORTHO.
   D) OSNAP.
   E) SNAP.

4. When drawing in isometric mode, what key(s) do you press to toggle among the isometric planes?

   A) ctrl-P
   B) F3
   C) F5
   D) ctrl-I
   E) alt-P

5. By default, ELLIPSES are drawn in isometric orientation. True/False

6. Which of the following OSNAP modes will not work on ELLIPSES?

   A) CENter
   B) QUAdrant
   C) TANgent
   D) NEArest
   E) All of the above work on Ellipses

7. When in isometric mode, the fillet command will default to drawing portions of ellipses rather than circles. True/False

Crosshatching for Detail and Effect

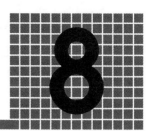

Objectives

1. Be able to apply crosshatching to objects in AutoCAD
2. Be able to correctly scale the crosshatching
3. Be able to edit the properties of crosshatching after it is applied
4. Be able to draw rectangles, general ellipses, polygons, and polylines

For anyone who has done extensive hand drafting, one of the most onerous tasks is crosshatching a large area. No matter how hard you try, the lines never come out just right and the pattern seems to shimmer due to the inconsistencies within it. However, the process of applying a hatch pattern to an area is very methodical. This is another area, like editing, where the power of a CAD program will become obvious. One thing computers do very well is to follow an algorithm and applying a pattern is very methodical.

Defining the Boundary

In order to fill an area with a pattern, you must first define what area you want to fill. This is done by drawing objects to enclose the desired area. You must have a closed area defined, however the objects can overlap without causing a problem. Figure 8.1 used a line and a circle to crosshatch a portion of the circle.

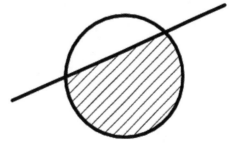

Figure 8.1

Notice that the line extends beyond the edge of the circle so that the area to be hatched is confined by part of the line and part of the circle.

Applying the Crosshatching

The command to actually apply crosshatching is BHATCH, which is located on the drawing toolbar. It will launch the dialog box shown in Figure 8.2.

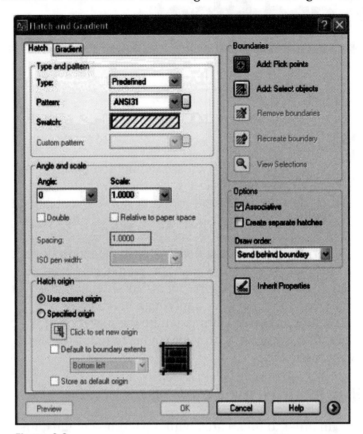

Figure 8.2

First, you should select what pattern you need to use. AutoCAD comes with 69 different patterns defined, and more can be downloaded via the Internet. If this weren't enough, you can apply a gradient fill to an area to let one color blend into another. The danger with that is many people go hog wild and start to pick all kinds of fancy patterns to "make the drawing look cool." An engineering drawing is a specific type designed to convey information. When you select a pattern, it should be representative of the material the object is constructed from. The most common materials in engineering and their pattern names in AutoCAD are shown in Figure 8.3.

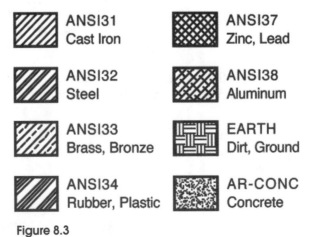

ANSI31 — Cast Iron
ANSI32 — Steel
ANSI33 — Brass, Bronze
ANSI34 — Rubber, Plastic
ANSI37 — Zinc, Lead
ANSI38 — Aluminum
EARTH — Dirt, Ground
AR-CONC — Concrete

Figure 8.3

If you want to look through the available patterns then instead of just dropping down the list of patterns, select the ellipsis (. . .) to the right of the pattern name and you will be shown thumbnails of the available patterns. To get a gradient pattern you must select the tab labeled "Gradient." Doing so will reveal the dialog box shown in Figure 8.4.

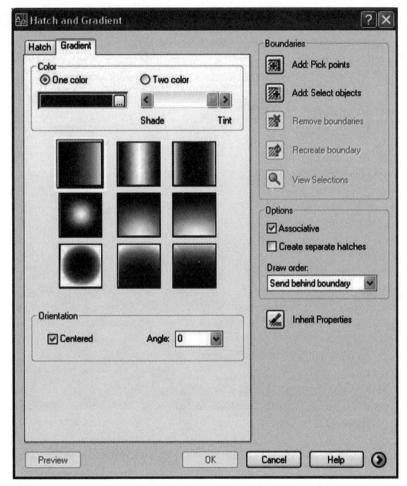

Figure 8.4

If you are using a regular hatch pattern, you need to decide on the relative pattern scale and the rotation angle that should be used. The ANSI patterns are defined as full scale patterns and therefore, if your drawing is intended to be plotted at full scale you should leave the scale at 1 (or close to it). If the drawing is to be plotted at another scale, then the scale factor should be adjusted to account for plot scale. Non-ANSI patterns are drawn at irregular scales and may or may not look good at a scale factor of 1 on a full sized drawing. Especially the patterns prefixed with "AR-," the scale should be adjusted to a rather small value (about 0.03) for full scale drawings. The patterns are shown rotated with a zero degree rotation; you should change the rotation angle to account for different parts or irregular boundaries if necessary.

Selecting the Pattern, Scale, and Angle will determine the appearance of the crosshatching; now all that remains is to select where the pattern should appear. The most common manner to select this is to use the Pick Points option and select a point internal to the area you wish to crosshatch. AutoCAD will trace a boundary comprised of objects (or portions thereof) that enclose the point you selected. It will also select all closed boundaries within that first boundary.

These interior boundaries are called "islands." AutoCAD can handle these in different ways. These can be selected by flying out the advanced portion of the dialog box. This is done by selecting the " > " sign in the lower right hand corner of the box. It will expand to look like Figure 8.5. Depending on the settings here they may or may not be crosshatched. You may select whether AutoCAD should ignore these islands,

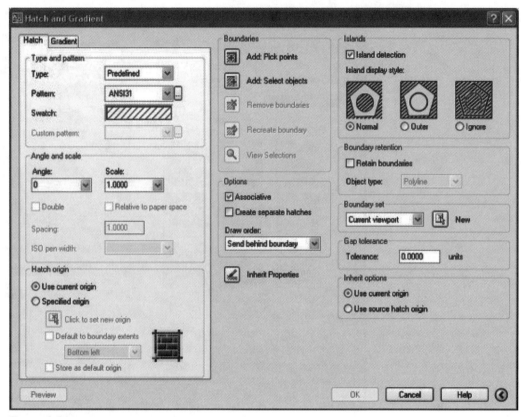

Figure 8.5

only crosshatch the outermost ring available, or alternate hatching and not hatching the rings.

One final option which is available to help you control which areas of your drawing are crosshatched is the Remove Islands button. This will allow you to remove any one closed loop, other than the outermost, from consideration. This button will activate once you have picked a point to identify the region for hatching.

Once you have the boundary selected and the Island Style selected, preview the resulting pattern by selecting the Preview button. If you want to make any changes, press enter or right click to return to the dialog box and edit the parameters as you need. Once the preview looks the way you want it to, select OK and the crosshatching will be applied to your drawing.

If you already have some crosshatching on your drawing which you would like to match, you may select the Inherit Properties button and select the existing hatching. The Pattern Name, Scale, and Angle will be filled in to match the existing hatch.

Associative Crosshatching

One nice feature of AutoCAD's crosshatching is the associative nature of the pattern. The crosshatching is truly associated with the objects which form its boundary. If you edit one of these boundary objects, AutoCAD will try to update the crosshatching to accommodate the new position. If it cannot (for instance, you erased one of the boundaries), then you will receive a warning that the associativity of the crosshatching was removed. This will sometimes yield unusual results. Reusing the initial circle and line figure, if the line is moved (via grips) to different positions you could get the following two figures shown in Figure 8.6.

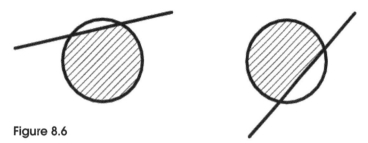

Figure 8.6

The figure on the left is what we would have expected, with the line moving farther up the circle the hatching expands to fill the new area, but the figure on the right is a bit different. That crosshatching has flipped from one side of the line to the other. The Line passed over the initial definition point of the crosshatching and thus, the area defined is now the portion of the circle shown.

Editing Existing Crosshatching

Once you have applied crosshatching, it is possible to make modifications in the pattern, scale, or angle of the hatching. The actual command to use is HATCHEDIT, however it is normally more convenient to double click the hatching which will launch the HATCHEDIT dialog box. This dialog box looks almost identical to the original apply hatch box shown earlier in the chapter. The only differences are in the buttons which are grayed out. You cannot relocate the hatching, thus the "Select Objects" and "Pick Points" buttons are not available.

Special Objects

AutoCAD supports several special objects, which similar to circles, act as one object when being edited or crosshatched. These can be drawn with a single command and have multiple grips available for editing once created.

Rectangles

Rectangles are drawn using the RECTANG command or the icon from the draw toolbar. You will be prompted for opposite corners of the rectangle and it will be created with horizontal and vertical sides.

```
Command: rectang
Specify first corner point or
      [Chamfer/Elevation/Fillet/Thickness/Width]:
Specify other corner point or [Dimensions]:
```

Ellipses

Ellipses are slightly more complicated than rectangles to draw. You use the ELLIPSE command or the icon. There are several options for specifying the major and minor diameters of the ellipse. By default you will select the ends of one of the axes and then one end of the second axis. Depending on the relative size, the first may be the major or the minor axis. Optionally, you can specify the center of the ellipse first, then specify one end point of each axis. It is also possible to draw an elliptical arc using the ELLIPSE command.

```
Command: ELLIPSE
Specify axis endpoint of ellipse or [Arc/Center]:
Specify other endpoint of axis:
Specify distance to other axis or [Rotation]:
Command: ELLIPSE
Specify axis endpoint of ellipse or [Arc/Center]: C
Specify center of ellipse:
Specify endpoint of axis:
Specify distance to other axis or [Rotation]:
Command: ELLIPSE
Specify axis endpoint of ellipse or [Arc/Center]: a
Specify axis endpoint of elliptical arc or [Center]:
Specify other endpoint of axis:
Specify distance to other axis or [Rotation]:
Specify start angle or [Parameter]:
Specify end angle or [Parameter/Included angle]:
```

Polygons

Equilateral polygons are frequent objects needed on engineering drawings. Squares appear in many designs and hexagons are very common on bolts and nuts. To draw a polygon you use the POLYGON command or the icon. You will be asked how many sides you want your polygon to have. You may choose any integer between 3 and 1024, inclusive. You must then locate the polygon on the drawing by either specifying the location of the endpoints of one edge or the location of the characteristic circle associated with the polygon and whether the polygon is to be inscribed in the circle or circumscribed about the circle as shown in Figure 8.7.

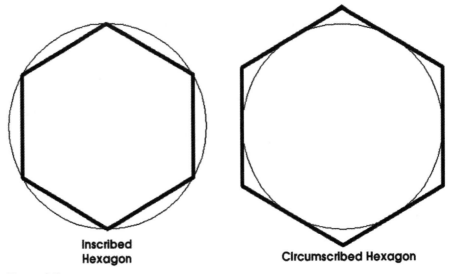

Inscribed Hexagon

Circumscribed Hexagon

Figure 8.7

```
Command: POLYGON
Enter number of sides <6>: 8
Specify center of polygon or [Edge]: E
Specify first endpoint of edge:
Specify second endpoint of edge:
Command: POLYGON
Enter number of sides <8>: 6
Specify center of polygon or [Edge]:
Enter an option [Inscribed in circle/Circumscribed about circle]
      <I>: I
Specify radius of circle:
Command: POLYGON
Enter number of sides <6>:
Specify center of polygon or [Edge]:
Enter an option [Inscribed in circle/Circumscribed about circle]
      <I>: C
Specify radius of circle:
```

Polylines

Polylines are really the granddaddy of all these special objects. A polyline is a collection of line segments on arcs which are grouped together into a single object in AutoCAD. Unlike other objects, each segment of a polyline can be assigned a width for screen display and plotting which is not related to the line weight parameter. The segments can even taper from one end to the other. Polylines can also be smoothed out by curve fitting using several different methods, each resulting in a different shape.

Polylines can be created in several ways, but the most common is with the PLINE command. When you use the pline command, you must initially pick the beginning point for the polyline and you will then be presented with the many options of the polyline command.

```
Command: pline

Specify start point:
Current line-width is 0.0000
Specify next point or [Arc/Halfwidth/Length/Undo/Width]: {pick
      point}
Specify next point or [Arc/Close/Halfwidth/Length/Undo/Width]:
      {pick point}
Specify next point or [Arc/Close/Halfwidth/Length/Undo/Width]:
      {pick point}
Specify next point or [Arc/Close/Halfwidth/Length/Undo/Width]:
      {pick point}
Specify next point or [Arc/Close/Halfwidth/Length/Undo/Width]:
      width
Specify starting width <0.0000>: .1

Specify ending width <0.1000>: .5

Specify next point or [Arc/Close/Halfwidth/Length/Undo/Width]:
      {pick point}
Specify next point or [Arc/Close/Halfwidth/Length/Undo/Width]:
      {pick point}
```

```
Specify next point or [Arc/Close/Halfwidth/Length/Undo/Width]:
     {pick point}
Specify next point or [Arc/Close/Halfwidth/Length/Undo/Width]:
     arc

Specify endpoint of arc or
[Angle/CEnter/CLose/Direction/Halfwidth/Line/Radius/Second pt/
     Undo/Width]: {pick point}
Specify endpoint of arc or
[Angle/CEnter/CLose/Direction/Halfwidth/Line/Radius/Second pt/
     Undo/Width]: {pick point}
Specify endpoint of arc or{pick point}
[Angle/CEnter/CLose/Direction/Halfwidth/Line/Radius/Second pt/
     Undo/Width]: center

Specify center point of arc: {pick point}
Specify endpoint of arc or [Angle/Length]: angle
Specify included angle: 60

Specify endpoint of arc or
[Angle/CEnter/CLose/Direction/Halfwidth/Line/Radius/Second pt/
     Undo/Width]: {pick point}
Specify endpoint of arc or
[Angle/CEnter/CLose/Direction/Halfwidth/Line/Radius/Second pt/
     Undo/Width]: close
```

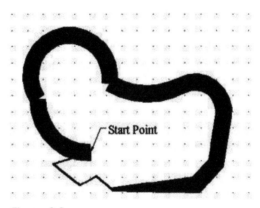

Figure 8.8

Notice that the fifth segment tapers from 0.1" wide to 0.5" wide. Following this the width stays at 0.5" unless you change it. Within the line segments, the corners are mitered to be smooth and within the tangent arcs segments there is a smooth blend from one to the other. When you specify a center or do something which makes the arc segments be non-tangent the corners are rough.

Revision Clouds

Revision clouds are normally used when reviewing or "redlining" a drawing. They are very efficient at calling attention to an area on the drawing so the original creator can see what you are flagging as good or bad on their drawing. A revision cloud is really nothing more than a polyline consisting of a series of convex arc segments to make it look like a cartoon cloud bubble. There are two styles of revision clouds in AutoCAD, normal and calligraphic (Figure 8.9).

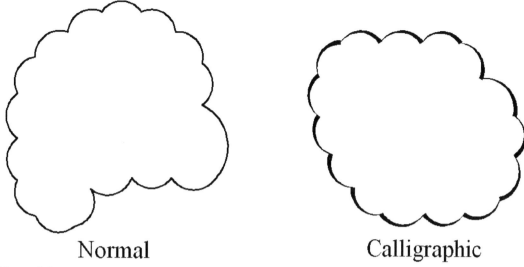

Normal   Calligraphic

Figure 8.9

To create a Revision Cloud you use the REVCLOUD command and simply sketch around the area you want to highlight or select a closed object you want to convert into a revision cloud. If you are sketching your own path the revision cloud will automatically close when you get back to the starting point (or within the maximum arc length set by the command parameters).

```
Command:  REVCLOUD
Minimum arc length: 0.5000    Maximum arc length: 0.5000    Style:
      Normal
Specify start point or [Arc length/Object/Style] <Object>: s
Select arc style [Normal/Calligraphy] <Normal>:c
Arc style = Calligraphy
Specify start point or [Arc length/Object/Style] <Object>:
Guide crosshairs along cloud path...
Revision cloud finished.
```

Review Questions

1. Care must be taken when drawing a boundary for a hatch pattern to insure that all line segments end precisely on the boundary of the hatching. True/False

2. The term for the areas within a larger boundary which do not get crosshatched is

   A) islands.
   B) omits.
   C) loops.
   D) boundaries.
   E) lakes.

3. By default, how will AutoCAD crosshatch a series of concentric circles?

   A) Crosshatch everything within the outermost circle.
   B) Crosshatch the innermost circle only.
   C) Crosshatch the area between the outermost and the second circle.
   D) Crosshatch alternating layers of circles.
   E) Request the user be more specific in which area will be crosshatched.

4. Which is larger, a hexagon drawn with the *Inscribe* or *Circumscribe* option using a radius 1 circle?

5. What is the maximum number of sides a polygon can have?

   A) 12
   B) 20
   C) 256
   D) 1024
   E) 65536

6. To draw a rectangle using the RECTANG command you pick the points for three corners, and AutoCAD will determine the fourth corner. True/False

7. To draw an elliptical arc, you must pick the center point for the arc. True/False

8. Polylines can have width, independent of the line weight set in AutoCAD. True/False

9. Polylines must be composed of straight line segments. True/False

10. All polylines must be closed, forming an irregular polygon. True/False

11. Arc segments on polylines must be tangent to the previous line segment. True/False

Dimensioning and Annotation of Drawings

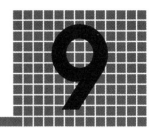

Objectives

1. To be able to apply dimensions to drawings
2. To be able to apply centerlines to a drawing using dimensioning
3. To be able to apply linear tolerances to drawings
4. To be able to apply geometric tolerances to drawings
5. To adjust the dimensioning style to account for different plotting scales

One of the major purposes of an engineering drawing is to document the design for construction. In order to actually build an object, it is necessary to know how big it will be. Thus, engineering drawings require dimensions. Hand in hand with dimensions are tolerances. To function correctly, tolerances are frequently necessary.

AutoCAD does semi-automatic dimensioning. It will apply dimensions in any manner the user tells it, without regard to proper style, however all the measurements will be correct. As can be seen from the toolbar shown in Figure 9.1, there are many options for applying dimensions in AutoCAD. In each case, you should have some idea about what your finished drawing should look like prior to applying dimensioning.

One point to make about the method AutoCAD uses to apply and calculate dimensions for a drawing. By default, AutoCAD creates dimensions that dynamically update if you edit the size or location of a feature on the drawing. This is controlled by a parameter in AutoCAD called DIMASSOC. This parameter has three valid settings: 0, 1, and 2. The setting of 0 will disable all the updating capability of the dimensions and remains in AutoCAD only to maintain backward compatibility. Use of mode 0 is not recommended. Mode 2 supports bi-directional associativity between model space and layout mode. This chapter assumes that you have set DIMASSOC to 2. If you are following along using AutoCAD and are getting different results than presented in the examples, check this setting.

Figure 9.1

79

Linear Dimensions

Linear dimensions comprise most of the dimensions for engineering drawings. They are defined by two points for the ends of the extension lines, one point for the locations of the dimension line, and an angle for the dimension line. (Remember to keep terminology correct, what is a dimension line, and what are extension lines.) Normally the dimension line angle will be either 0° (horizontal) or 90° (vertical) and this orientation can be inferred by the selection of the three points.

As an example, look at applying dimensions to the sloped line in Figure 9.2. In each case, the 1st and 2nd points were chosen the same, but the 3rd point selected determined whether the dimension was to be a horizontal one (the 3.5) or a vertical one (the 1.5).

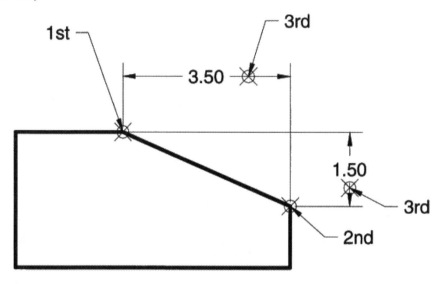

Figure 9.2

```
Command: _dimlinear
Specify first extension line origin or <select object>: {select
     point 1}
Specify second extension line origin: {select point 2}
Non-associative dimension created.
Specify dimension line location or [Mtext/Text/Angle/Horizontal/
     Vertical/Rotated]: {select point 3 on the 3.50 dimension}
Dimension text = 3.50
Command: _dimlinear
Specify first extension line origin or <select object>:{select
     point 1}
Specify second extension line origin: {select point 2}
Non-associative dimension created.
Specify dimension line location or [Mtext/Text/Angle/Horizontal/
     Vertical/Rotated]: {select point 3 on the 1.50 dimension}
Dimension text = 1.50
```

Notice that no options were selected to change from a horizontal to a vertical dimension. Prior to selecting the 3rd point, you may choose one of the available options, but in most cases, it is not necessary.

Aligned Dimensions

If you had wanted to dimension the actual length of the sloped face, then you would use an aligned dimension rather than a linear one. The result would be:

```
Command: dimaligned
Specify first extension line origin or <select object>:{select
     point 1}
Specify second extension line origin: {select point 2}
Non-associative dimension created.
Specify dimension line location or [Mtext/Text/Angle]: {select
     point 3}
Dimension text = 3.81
```

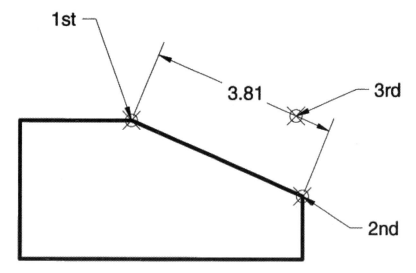

Figure 9.3

Radius and Diameter Dimensions

If you have an arc or a circle, then you should use either Radius (if it is an arc) or Diameter (if it is a full circle). The application of these dimensions is straight forward, but they open a virtual Pandora's box of options due to the presence or absence of centerlines. AutoCAD can be set to apply centerlines automatically when applying radius or diameter dimensions. An arc can be dimensioned with any of the following centerline combinations:

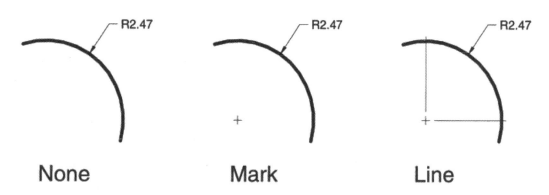

Figure 9.4

It is possible to have AutoCAD simply draw the centerlines without applying either a radius or diameter dimension by using the Center option and selecting the arc or circle.

These are controlled through something referred to as Dimension Styles. Like Text Styles they are a set of parameters used to define the appearance of dimensions. There are 70 different settings which affect the appearance of dimensions. These are all controlled through a series of dialog boxes accessed via the DIMSTYLE command. Most of the settings will be established in the base template file and you will not have to modify them, however a few are worth noting in detail. The initial dialog box is shown in Figure 9.5.

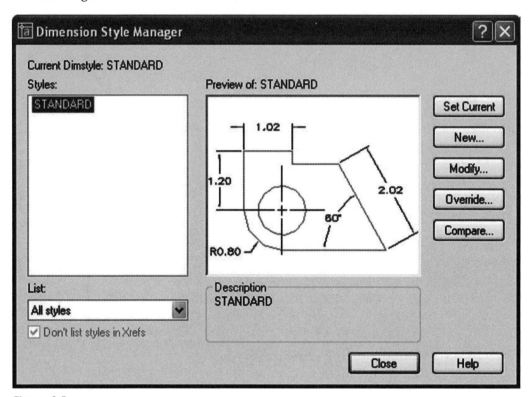

Figure 9.5

All the settings can be accessed by choosing modify. This will open a new dialog box with six tabs. The settings that you may want to adjust are Center marks (under the Lines and Arrows tab), Text Alignment (under the Text tab), Scale for dimensioning features and Fine Tuning (under the Fit tab), and Precision (under the Primary Units tab).

Center Marks: This setting controls how the Radius, Diameter and Center options draw center marks. If used with the Radius or Diameter options the center marks become part of the dimension, however if used with the Center option they are independent objects and can be modified as such.

Text Alignment: Probably does not need to be modified, since the engineering standard of Unidirectional is the default.

Scale for Dimensioning Features: This is where you would account for a plotting scale other than 1 to 1.

Fine Tuning: Normally AutoCAD will attempt to place the dimension directly in the middle of the dimension line. If you would rather have the text placed at the location of the 3rd selection point, then choose "Place text manually when dimensioning."

Precision: This controls the number of decimal places AutoCAD uses for dimensions.

Angular Dimensioning

Angular dimensions can be applied to an arc, two points on a circle, two lines, or three points and will measure the angle associated with the objects.

Baseline and Continue Dimensioning

Baseline and continuation dimensioning are really just specialized forms of linear dimensioning. With a baseline dimension AutoCAD will hold the first extension line location in memory and repeatedly ask you for a second extension line location, drawing a dimension for the first to each successive second. Continue holds the second extension line in memory, transferring it to be a first and then prompts you for a new second extension line location.

Closely related to Continue dimensioning is Quick Dimensioning. Quick dimensioning prompts you to select the geometry you want to dimension. This can be done with any of the selection set techniques discussed for editing. Once you have everything selected that you want to dimension, press return and you can drag either a horizontal or vertical dimension in place for all of the objects concurrently. It is a neat option without a lot of practical applications.

Leaders

Leaders are a very flexible method for applying general notes to specific features on a drawing. They are very useful for thread notes, knurls, and chamfers. The leader begins on the feature to be dimensioned and ends at the location of the note.

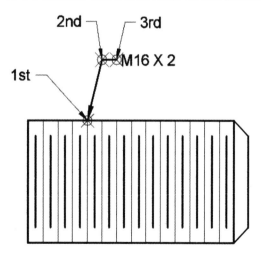

Figure 9.6

```
Command: _qleader
Specify first leader point, or [Settings] <Settings>:
Specify next point:
Specify next point:

Specify text width <0.0000>: {Press Enter}

Enter first line of annotation text <Mtext>: M16 X 2
Enter next line of annotation text:
```

Editing of Dimensions

Dimensioning styles are useful, but more often changes need to be made on one particular dimension, not globally on all dimensions. To do this you need to modify properties on the individual dimension. The same six categories are available for editing as were in the Dimension Styles, but these properties apply only to the dimension selected. If you need to change the text height for one particular dimension or the center mark style of one, you would modify the properties for that dimension using the Modify Properties command. The resulting properties box is shown in Figure 9.7.

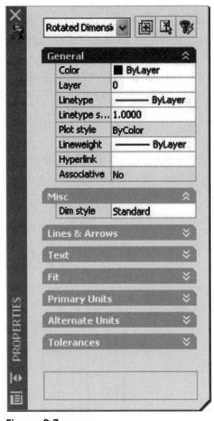

Figure 9.7

Linear Tolerances

From an engineering drawing point of view, one of the most useful applications of editing dimensions is to apply linear tolerances.

To apply the tolerance shown in Figure 9.8, you must first make sure the part is drawn **exactly** to the correct size. Do not try to draw a part without snap on and then apply dimensions to it, much less toleranced dimensions.

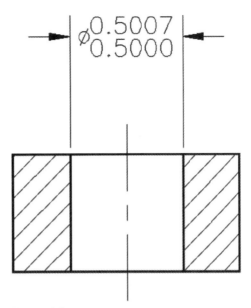

Figure 9.8

Apply a dimension of 0.5000 in the normal fashion. Then perform a modify properties operation on this dimension. Under the Tolerance sections are three parameters which need to be checked. The dialog box is shown in Figure 9.9.

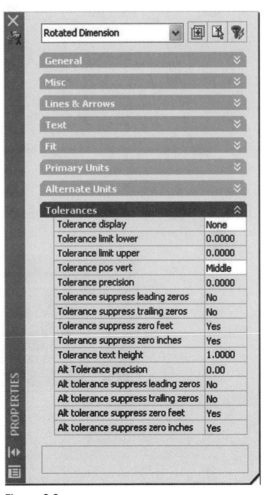

Figure 9.9

The tolerance display should be set to Limits form in order to display the tolerance correctly on the drawing. Setting it to Symmetrical or Deviation will tolerance the dimension, but it is not in the engineering standard format. Once that has been switched to Limits, then the "Tolerance limit lower" and "Tolerance limit upper" will ungray and you should enter the deviations from the basic size here. The "Tolerance Limit Lower" will be subtracted from the basic dimension to obtain the lower limit and the "Tolerance Limit Upper" will be added to the basic dimension to get the upper limit. For this dimension, the Tolerance Limit Upper should be set to 0.0007, and the Tolerance Limit Lower should be set to 0.0000.

Geometric Tolerances

Linear tolerances are only half of the picture. Geometric tolerances specify not the size of a feature, but the shape and orientation. AutoCAD has a special mode for applying geometric tolerances. The dialog box (Figure 9.10) guides you through the process very well.

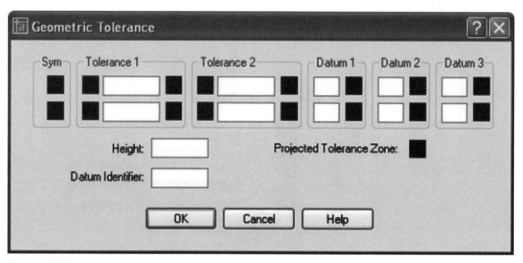

Figure 9.10

If you click on the "Sym" section, you will get another box of possible symbols shown in Figure 9.11. You just select the correct geometric tolerance symbol and it will be inserted at the correct location in the callout box.

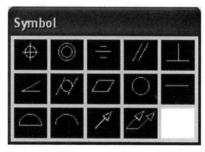

Figure 9.11

The square in front of the tolerance zone is for a diameter symbol "Ø" and by clicking on it you can toggle the display of that symbol. The box after Tolerance zone is for Material Condition specification (Figure 9.12).

Figure 9.12

Once you get all the specifications entered into the box, select OK and you will be able to drag the box into place on the drawing. Notice that this does not draw a leader, it just draws the feature control frame.

Example:

Create the following annotations on a drawing.

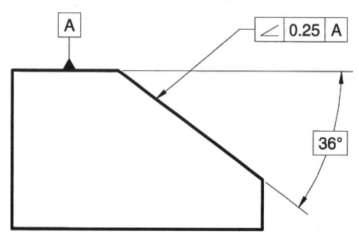

Figure 9.13

Step 1: Draw the figure.

Step 2: Place an angular dimension between the top surface and the sloped surface. Do not worry about the basic dimension indicator for the moment.

Step 3: Add the basic dimension indicator to the angular dimension by selecting it and doing a modify properties. Under the Tolerance section select the "Tolerance Display" and choose "Basic." This will place a box around the dimension indicating that it is a basic dimension.

Step 4: Add the datum reference to the upper surface.

Step 4A: Turn ortho on and select the Quick Leader icon from the dimension toolbar (or use QLEADER). Before selecting any points go into the setting option. You will see a dialog box like the one shown in Figure 9.14.

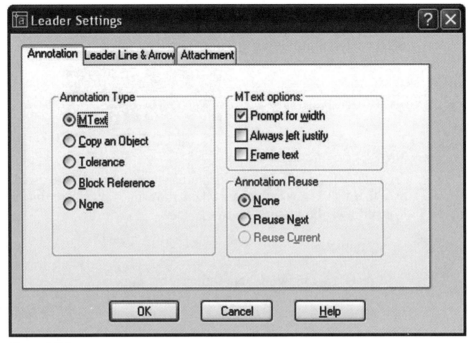

Figure 9.14

Set the Annotation type to None and on the "Leader Line & Arrow" tab select "Datum Triangle Filled" and select OK. Now pick a point on the upper surface and one directly above it. Then press return to complete the Datum Leader.

Step 4B: Select the Tolerance option from the Dimension Toolbar and enter just the letter "A" in the lower "Datum identifier" position. Select OK and drag the datum identifier into place. (You may have to get it close and then move it exactly into place using OSNAP midpoint on the box and endpoint on the leader.)

Step 5: Create the Feature Control Frame. Return to the Tolerance icon on the toolbar and enter the information for the Feature Control Frame as shown in Figure 9.15. Then select OK and drag it into place.

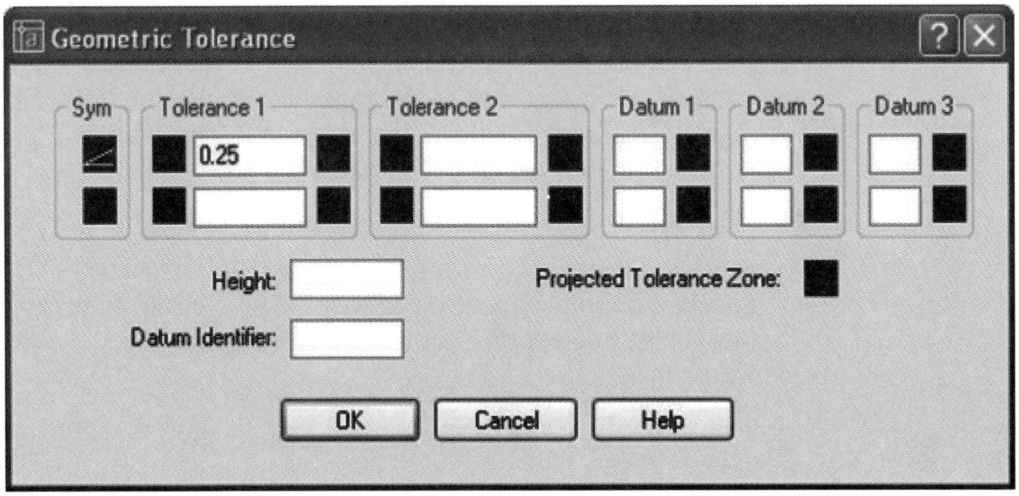

Figure 9.15

Step 6: Add the final leader. Select the Quick Leader option and return to the settings option. Reset the arrowhead to a normal Closed Filled arrow and apply the leader beginning on the sloped surface and ending at the Feature Control Frame.

Review Questions

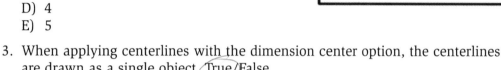

1. The dimension shown to the right is

   A) horizontal.
   B) vertical.
   C) aligned.
   D) rotated.
   E) none of the above.

2. To apply the dimension shown, how many points had to be selected?

   A) 1
   B) 2
   C) 3
   D) 4
   E) 5

3. When applying centerlines with the dimension center option, the centerlines are drawn as a single object. True/False

4. AutoCAD will determine whether a dimension line should be horizontal or vertical based on the locations of the points selected to draw it. True/False

5. If you were working on a drawing which was to be plotted at a scale other than 1 to 1, you should change the text height and arrow size under dimension styles to make things look correct. True/False

6. Quick dimensioning will apply horizontal and vertical dimensions to a drawing automatically. True/False

7. The distance from the object to the dimension line is determined automatically by AutoCAD. True/False

8. When drawing leaders

   A) you begin at the text, place the elbow, and end at the desired feature.
   B) you begin at the text and go directly to the feature. AutoCAD will automatically add the elbow.
   C) you begin at the feature, draw the elbow, and end by the text location.
   D) select an existing feature and then the text object. AutoCAD will connect them with a leader.
   E) select an existing text object and then the feature. AutoCAD will connect them with a leader.

9. If the basic size of a feature is 1.00 and the desired linear tolerance zone is 1.0015–1.0046, what would you set the value of "Dimension Limit Upper" to in the modify properties box?

   A) 1.0046
   B) 0.0046
   C) −0.0046
   D) 0.0031
   E) 0.0015

10. If the basic size of a feature is 1.00 and the desired linear tolerance zone is 1.0015–1.0046, what would you set the value of "Dimension Limit Lower" to in the modify properties box?

   A) 1.0015
   B) 0.0015
   C) –0.0015
   D) –0.0031
   E) –0.0046

11. To apply a datum mark to a feature in AutoCAD, you should

   A) use the DATUM command.
   B) use the QLEADER command.
   C) draw a 3 sided polygon and add the line manually.
   D) use the GEOTOL command.
   E) none of the above.

Merging of Files, Blocks, and External References

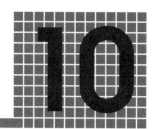

Objectives

1. Be able to create a Block in AutoCAD
2. Be able to insert a Block, from disk or memory, into the current drawing
3. Be able to drag objects from one open drawing into another
4. Be able to place a bitmapped graphic image on an AutoCAD drawing
5. Be able to use files as external references

As stated earlier, one of the advantages of CAD is that you never have to draw anything twice. Once you have drawn something in one place, you can simply copy it to another location and avoid the time and effort of recreating it. As long as it is within the same file this works, but between files it requires a different approach. One of these different approaches is to use Blocks to copy items. A block is simply a collection of objects grouped together and given a name. This group effectively becomes a new object type which can be placed in the drawing as if it were any of the simple objects we have examined so far.

Creation of Blocks

The hardest part of block creation is simply drawing the objects you want to group together. These are drawn just as if you were trying to draw the symbol on the drawing normally, with no concept of making a block of it. This statement is not quite true, since there are a few things that you can, but do not have to, consider. These deal with putting the objects on the correct layer so that they will behave as you want in subsequent insertions of the block.

 The command to create the block is BLOCK and it will launch the dialog box shown in Figure 10.1.

The first requirement is that you specify a unique name to identify the block. This name will be the reference for the block in the future. You must also select the objects you want to include in the block. This is the same as forming a selection set for editing. Finally, you must select a Base Point. To understand this we need to look toward the future a little and see how the block will be used.

If you have created a block of the end view for a hex nut, when you place the nut on a drawing you will do so by picking a point to locate the hex nut. The question is, "What point will that be on the hex nut?" Will it be the center of the hole? Will it be the center of one side? Will it be the left corner of the nut? Any of these are possibilities, so when the block is made, you must specify the base point so that AutoCAD will know which point to reference when inserting the block.

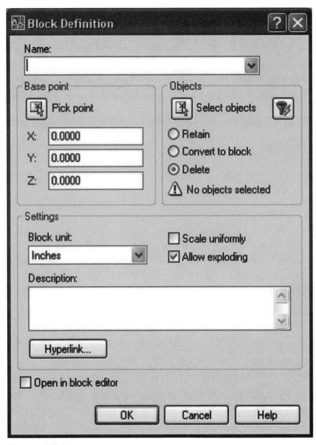

Figure 10.1

To actually select the base point you can either enter the coordinates directly in the spaces provided on the dialog box, or select the Pick Point button and actually select the point on your drawing.

Once these have been selected, selecting OK will create the block. Depending on the option selected under the Objects section, the original will either be deleted, retained, or converted to a block.

Inserting a Block

 With a block defined we can now discuss placing the block elsewhere in the drawing. The command to place a block in a drawing is INSERT. As usual, you will see a dialog box appear (Figure 10.2). There are a few interesting features that are available when inserting blocks. They are not just exact carbon copies of the original definition but they can be scaled larger or smaller (independently in X, Y, and even Z) or they can be rotated from the original definition. This gives you a lot of flexibility since you don't want to have to draw every bolt you might need in all its orientations, you want to draw it once and then block and insert it as needed at whatever rotation angle each occurrence requires.

There is also a Browse... button. It is possible to insert an entire file into your current drawing. The whole file will become a single block in the current drawing and can be moved, scaled, or rotated as one unit. If you want to be able to operate on individual objects within that block, check the Explode box in the lower left corner. This will force the block to appear not as a single unit, but as a bunch of individual objects.

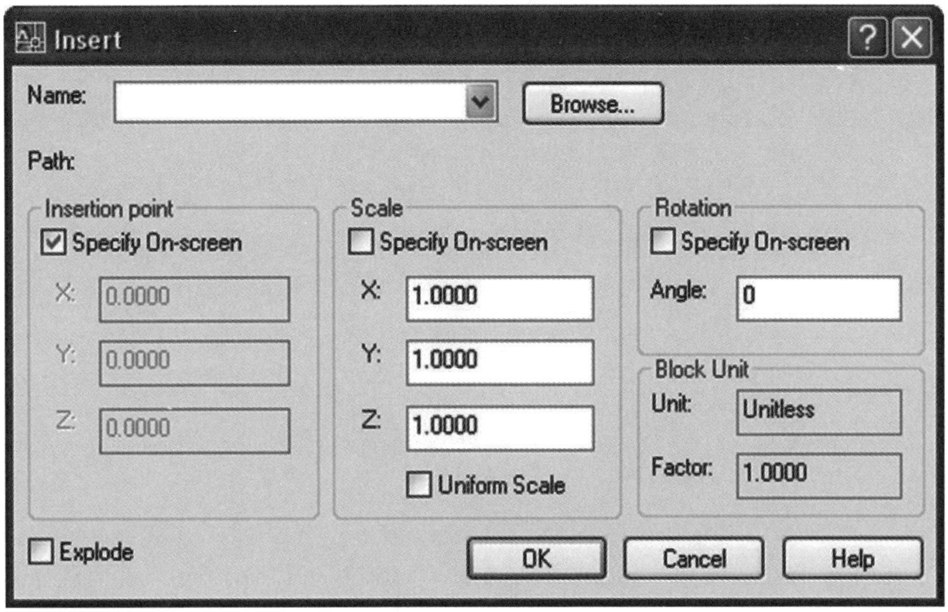

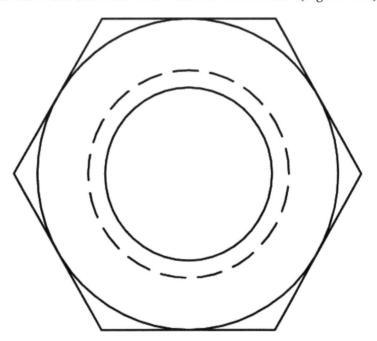

Figure 10.2

Example: Draw the end view of a 1-12UNF-2B hex nut (Figure 10.3).

Figure 10.3

Set the snap and grid for the drawing. Also set the current layer to Visible.

```
Command: snap
Specify snap spacing or [ON/OFF/Aspect/Rotate/Style/Type]
     <0.5000>: 0.125
Command: grid
Specify grid spacing(X) or [ON/OFF/Snap/Aspect] <0.5000>: 0.25
```

Draw the circle for the major diameter.

```
Command: circle
Specify center point for circle or [3P/2P/Ttr (tan tan radius)]:
     1,1
Specify radius of circle or [Diameter]: 0.5
```

Create the minor diameter by offsetting the major diameter by the pitch.

```
Command: offset
Specify offset distance or [Through] <1.0000>: 1/12
Select object to offset or <exit>: {select the circle}
Specify point on side to offset: {select a point inside the
     circle}
Select object to offset or <exit>:
```

Change the major diameter circle from visible to layer hidden by selecting it using grips and changing the layer via the dropdown list of layers. This step does not give any command line feedback and is, therefore, not noticeable in the command stream.

Draw the outer circle of the nut. Remember that for a normal hex nut the outer circle has a diameter of 1.5 times the major diameter of the thread.

```
Command: circle
Specify center point for circle or [3P/2P/Ttr (tan tan radius)]:
     1,1

Specify radius of circle or [Diameter] <0.5000>: 0.75
```

Add the surrounding hexagon.

```
Command: polygon
Enter number of sides <4>: 6
Specify center of polygon or [Edge]: 1,1
Enter an option [Inscribed in circle/Circumscribed about circle]
     <I>: c
Specify radius of circle: .75
```

Make the block using the dialog box settings shown in Figure 10.4.

```
Command: block
Select objects: Specify opposite corner: 4 found
Select objects:
```

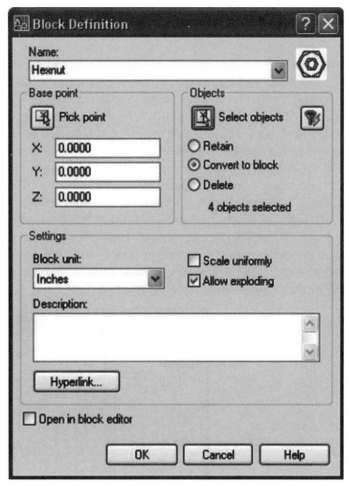

Figure 10.4

Now that the block is made, we can insert it.

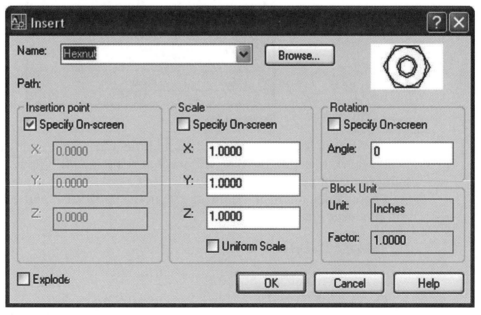

Figure 10.5

Divide and Measure

Two other commands which can be used to place a block in a drawing are DIVIDE and MEASURE. The normal function of these commands is to place point objects along other objects, thus giving you uniform markings. Both commands execute using the same format, the results are just slightly different. When using the DIVIDE command you will be asked for the number of segments you want and the resulting object will be marked such that all the resulting marks are uniformly spaced along the entire length of the object. The MEASURE command will ask for a spacing between marks and the marks will begin at one end of the object and be placed at the spacing you specified. In this case the distance from the last mark to the end may be less than the spacing, depending on the length of the object to begin with.

Before demonstrating these commands, some attention must be given to POINT objects. In AutoCAD, point objects can be configured to take a variety of shapes. The choices are shown in a dialog box using the DDPTYPE command or by selecting the Point Style... option from the Format pulldown. The resulting dialog box is shown in Figure 10.6.

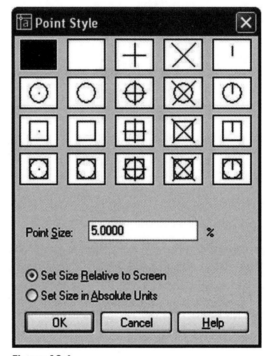

Figure 10.6

The default is a single dot as shown in the upper right hand corner. To make the points show up better, the type will be changed to an "X" (Row 1, column 4) for the following example.

The command stream below shows both the DIVIDE and MEASURE command and produces Figure 10.7.

```
Command: divide

Select object to divide:
Enter the number of segments or [Block]: 5

Command: measure
Select object to measure:
Specify length of segment or [Block]: 1.2
```

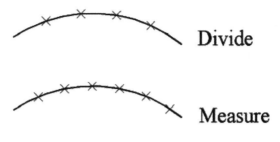

Divide

Measure

Figure 10.7

If you observe closely, you will notice that in both cases the commands offered the option of [Block] when specifying an interval. Using this option will prompt you for an existing block and it will insert that block along the object instead of the points.

For example, suppose you wanted to place hex nuts uniformly along a circle in order to create a bolt circle. The path would be a circle of the correct diameter. The command stream shows the creation of the path and the subsequent addition of the nuts.

```
Command: CIRCLE Specify center point for circle or [3P/2P/Ttr
     (tan tan radius)]:
Specify radius of circle or [Diameter]:
Command: divide
Select object to divide:
Enter the number of segments or [Block]: block
Enter name of block to insert: hexnut
Align block with object? [Yes/No] <Y>: no
Enter the number of segments: 5
```

Drag and Drop

If you want to move a portion of one drawing into another, there are several strategies. You can use the command WBLOCK to write a portion of your current drawing to disk as a separate drawing. This will allow you to insert that disk file in another drawing or just allow you to split a drawing into smaller pieces. While this process works to transfer objects, if that is your only goal, there are easier methods.

If you open both the files which contain the objects you want to move and the file that you want to move them into, the objects can be selected with grips and then you can drag them from one drawing into another. Highlight all the objects you want to move and then select one of the grips using the right mouse button. Hold the right button down and you can drag the items to a new location within that file, or into the adjacent file. When you release the right button, you will be prompted with the popup menu shown in Figure 10.8. You can copy the objects or make a block of them in the new file.

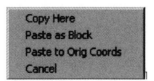

Figure 10.8

AutoCAD Design Center

One additional method of drag and drop options for blocks (and other items as well) is AutoCAD's Design Center. Rather than open two drawings and drag items from one to the other, you can open the design center and a drag block directly to the current drawing. This is particularly useful, since AutoCAD comes with several sets of pre-defined blocks which are ready to be dropped into your drawings. To activate the design center go to the Tools menu and select it (Figure 10.9) or press "Ctrl-2."

The design center will appear on the left side of the drawing with two areas. One is a directory structure of your disk drive and the other a preview pane to see the items available to be dragged and dropped.

Under the Main AutoCAD directory you should have a samples directory and under that a Design Center directory. This directory has blocks for kitchen layout, electric circuit layout, space

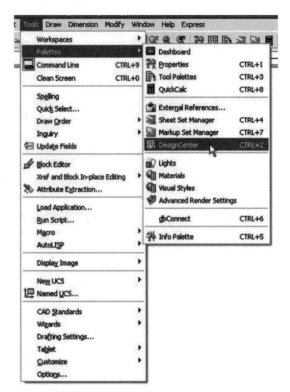

Figure 10.9

planning for house design, piping, welding, and many others. To use one of the blocks in a drawing, expand that drawing and select the blocks icon. The preview pane will now show a thumbnail of the blocks which are available for drag and drop. The Basic Electronics blocks are shown in Figure 10.10. To put a battery on your drawing simply drag the battery thumbnail to your drawing and release the left mouse button.

Windows Cut and Paste

You can also use the traditional Windows Cut and Paste to copy objects to the clipboard in one drawing and to paste them to the drawing area in another.

External References

To a beginning student there will appear to be very little difference in effect by using either External References or Blocks, but the effect in AutoCAD is substantial. The major difference is in the ability to update multiple drawings easily and to manage file sizes more effectively. Each has its place and used properly, the combination can be a very powerful tool to increase your productivity.

An external reference is a pointer to a separate drawing file which is to be drawn on top of the current file. Each time the current file is reloaded or printed, the pointer is checked and the contents of that external file (whatever they may be at the time) are super-imposed on the drawing. Thus, if the contents of the external file change,

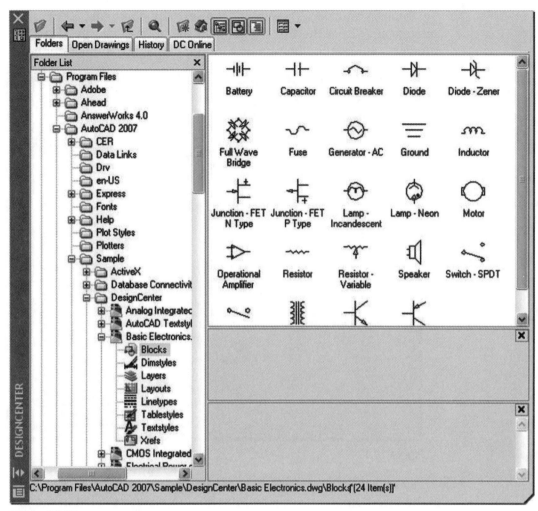

C:\Program Files\AutoCAD 2007\Sample\DesignCenter\Basic Electronics.dwg\Blocks (24 Item(s))

Figure 10.10

the superimposed image will also change. This can be used as a very effective method to make changes to one file (the reference file) which will be reflected in all the files which reference it. Consider a company logo that appears on all drawings done by that engineering firm. If there is a change in the logo, all you would have to do is to update the logo file and all your drawings would be updated automatically the next time you opened them. Another advantage is that file sizes will generally be smaller than when you use external references instead of blocks.

The down side of external references is file management. With blocks a drawing is completely self contained. The drawing file can be transported anywhere and it will open, intact. With an external reference, you not only have to transport both the base drawing and the reference, but the reference file must have the same path relative to the drawing file for it to be found. (You can tell AutoCAD to ignore path, but you must think about this at the time or making the reference).

To place an external reference you use the command XREF or choose "External Reference..." from the Insert pulldown menu. You will be asked to select a file for reference and then be presented with the dialog box shown in Figure 10.11.

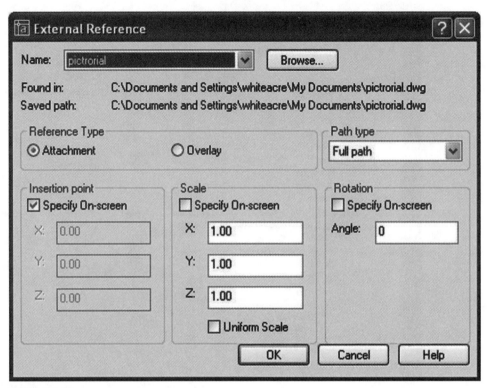

Figure 10.11

By selecting OK, the reference file will be placed on the current drawing according to the insertion point, scale and rotation you have selected in the dialog box.

Raster Images

One final class of things which can be added to an AutoCAD drawing are external raster (bitmapped) images. If you have a TIFF, GIF, JPEG, etc. file you would like to include on a drawing (again a company logo is a good example) then AutoCAD will allow you to reference this file in much the same way as an external reference. And like an external reference, the raster file must be transported along with the drawing for it to load correctly on a different computer.

To include a raster image use the IMAGEATTACH command on the Insert pulldown, and select "Raster Image..." You will be asked to select the image file from disk and will be presented with a dialog box similar to the External Reference box. Upon completing of the command your image will be included in your drawing.

Review Questions

1. To create a block you must specify which of the following?

   A) Insertion Base Point
   B) Rotation angle
   C) Objects to be blocked
   D) A and C
   E) A, B, and C

2. When you insert a block, all the objects within that block come in on the layer on which they were originally created. True/False

3. What option will cause a block to come into a drawing as individual objects, rather than the composite block?

   A) Separate
   B) Individual
   C) Unblock
   D) Explode
   E) This is the default, it requires no option

4. What command will place points on an object at user specified fixed intervals, regardless of the size of the object?

   A) POINT
   B) DIVIDE
   C) MEASURE
   D) INSERT
   E) SPACE

5. The DIVIDE command will separate an object into multiple objects. True/False

6. To drag and drop an object from one drawing to another you should

   A) use the MOVE command.
   B) use the DRAG command.
   C) use Grips and drag the object with the right mouse button.
   D) use Grips and drag the object with the left mouse button.
   E) use the Block command.

7. What key sequence will activate the Design Center?

   A) F4
   B) ctrl-F4
   C) alt-C
   D) alt-D
   E) ctrl-2

8. Using external references instead of Block/Insert will generally reduce your file size. True/False

9. One file may be referenced externally by many other files. True/False

10. When transferring a file with a raster image in it, you must also transfer the file from which the raster image came. True/False

AutoCAD Command Aliases

Alias	Command	Alias	Command
3A	3DARRAY	-CH	CHANGE
3DMIRROR	MIRROR3D	CHA	CHAMFER
3DNavigate	3DWALK	CHK	CHECKSTANDARDS
3DO	3DORBIT	CLI	COMMANDLINE
3DW	3DWALK	COL	COLOR
3F	3DFACE	COLOUR	COLOR
3M	3DMOVE	CO	COPY
3P	3DPOLY	CP	COPY
3R	3DROTATE	CT	CTABLESTYLE
A	ARC	CYL	CYLINDER
AC	BACTION	D	DIMSTYLE
ADC	ADCENTER	DAL	DIMALIGNED
AECTOACAD	-ExportToAutoCAD	DAN	DIMANGULAR
AA	AREA	DAR	DIMARC
AL	ALIGN	JOG	DIMJOGGED
3AL	3DALIGN	DBA	DIMBASELINE
AP	APPLOAD	DBC	DBCONNECT
AR	ARRAY	DC	ADCENTER
-AR	-ARRAY	DCE	DIMCENTER
ATT	ATTDEF	DCENTER	ADCENTER
-ATT	-ATTDEF	DCO	DIMCONTINUE
ATE	ATTEDIT	DDA	DIMDISASSOCIATE
-ATE	-ATTEDIT	DDI	DIMDIAMETER
ATTE	-ATTEDIT	DED	DIMEDIT
B	BLOCK	DI	DIST
-B	-BLOCK	DIV	DIVIDE
BC	BCLOSE	DJO	DIMJOGGED
BE	BEDIT	DLI	DIMLINEAR
BH	HATCH	DO	DONUT
BO	BOUNDARY	DOR	DIMORDINATE
-BO	-BOUNDARY	DOV	DIMOVERRIDE
BR	BREAK	DR	DRAWORDER
BS	BSAVE	DRA	DIMRADIUS
BVS	BVSTATE	DRE	DIMREASSOCIATE
C	CIRCLE	DRM	DRAWINGRECOVERY
CAM	CAMERA	DS	DSETTINGS
CH	PROPERTIES	DST	DIMSTYLE

Alias	Command	Alias	Command
DT	TEXT	MA	MATCHPROP
DV	DVIEW	MAT	MATERIALS
E	ERASE	ME	MEASURE
ED	DDEDIT	MI	MIRROR
EL	ELLIPSE	ML	MLINE
ER	EXTERNALREFERENCES	MO	PROPERTIES
EX	EXTEND	MS	MSPACE
EXIT	QUIT	MSM	MARKUP
EXP	EXPORT	MT	MTEXT
EXT	EXTRUDE	MV	MVIEW
F	FILLET	NORTH	GEOGRAPHICLOCATION
FI	FILTER	NORTHDIR	GEOGRAPHICLOCATION
FSHOT	FLATSHOT	O	OFFSET
G	GROUP	OP	OPTIONS
-G	-GROUP	ORBIT	3DORBIT
GD	GRADIENT	OS	OSNAP
GEO	GEOGRAPHICLOCATION	-OS	-OSNAP
GR	DDGRIPS	P	PAN
H	HATCH	-P	-PAN
-H	-HATCH	PA	PASTESPEC
HE	HATCHEDIT	PARAM	BPARAMETER
HI	HIDE	PARTIALOPEN	-PARTIALOPEN
I	INSERT	PE	PEDIT
-I	-INSERT	PL	PLINE
IAD	IMAGEADJUST	PO	POINT
IAT	IMAGEATTACH	POL	POLYGON
ICL	IMAGECLIP	PR	PROPERTIES
IM	IMAGE	PRCLOSE	PROPERTIESCLOSE
-IM	-IMAGE	PROPS	PROPERTIES
IMP	IMPORT	PRE	PREVIEW
IN	INTERSECT	PRINT	PLOT
INF	INTERFERE	PS	PSPACE
IO	INSERTOBJ	PSOLID	POLYSOLID
J	JOIN	PTW	PUBLISHTOWEB
L	LINE	PU	PURGE
LA	LAYER	-PU	-PURGE
-LA	-LAYER	PYR	PYRAMID
LE	QLEADER	QC	QUICKCALC
LEN	LENGTHEN	R	REDRAW
LI	LIST	RA	REDRAWALL
LINEWEIGHT	LWEIGHT	RC	RENDERCROP
LO	-LAYOUT	RE	REGEN
LS	LIST	REA	REGENALL
LT	LINETYPE	REC	RECTANG
-LT	-LINETYPE	REG	REGION
LTYPE	LINETYPE	REN	RENAME
-LTYPE	-LINETYPE	-REN	-RENAME
LTS	LTSCALE	REV	REVOLVE
LW	LWEIGHT	RO	ROTATE
M	MOVE	RP	RENDERPRESETS

Alias	Command	Alias	Command
RPR	RPREF	TOL	TOLERANCE
RR	RENDER	TOR	TORUS
RW	RENDERWIN	TP	TOOLPALETTES
S	STRETCH	TR	TRIM
SC	SCALE	TS	TABLESTYLE
SCR	SCRIPT	UC	UCSMAN
SE	DSETTINGS	UN	UNITS
SEC	SECTION	-UN	-UNITS
SET	SETVAR	UNI	UNION
SHA	SHADEMODE	V	VIEW
SL	SLICE	-V	-VIEW
SN	SNAP	VP	DDVPOINT
SO	SOLID	-VP	VPOINT
SP	SPELL	VS	VSCURRENT
SPL	SPLINE	VSM	VISUALSTYLES
SPLANE	SECTIONPLANE	-VSM	-VISUALSTYLES
SPE	SPLINEDIT	W	WBLOCK
SSM	SHEETSET	-W	-WBLOCK
ST	STYLE	WE	WEDGE
STA	STANDARDS	X	EXPLODE
SU	SUBTRACT	XA	XATTACH
T	MTEXT	XB	XBIND
-T	-MTEXT	-XB	-XBIND
TA	TABLET	XC	XCLIP
TB	TABLE	XL	XLINE
TH	THICKNESS	XR	XREF
TI	TILEMODE	-XR	-XREF
TO	TOOLBAR	Z	ZOOM

Standard AutoCAD Fonts

The following fonts are standard with AutoCAD. To use one of these fonts you must use the STYLE command and assign the given font to a text style. Any standard Windows font can also be used in a similar manner.

Complex	A B C D E F G H I J K L M N O P Q R S T U V W X Y Z ! @ # $ % ^ & * ( ) ~ _ + | < > ? : " { }
GothicE	𝕬 𝕭 𝕮 𝕯 𝕰 𝕱 𝕲 𝕳 𝕴 𝕵 𝕶 𝕷 𝕸 𝕹 𝕺 𝕻 𝕼 𝕽 𝕾 𝕿 𝖀 𝖁 𝖂 𝖃 𝖄 𝖅 ! @ # $ % ^ & * ( ) ~ _ + | < > ? : " { }
GothicG	𝕬 𝕭 𝕮 𝕯 𝕰 𝕱 𝕲 𝕳 𝕴 𝕵 𝕶 𝕷 𝕸 𝕹 𝕺 𝕻 𝕼 𝕽 𝕾 𝕿 𝖀 𝖁 𝖂 𝖃 𝖄 𝖅 ! @ # $ % ^ & * ( ) ~ _ + | < > ? : " { }
GothicI	𝕬 𝕭 𝕮 𝕯 𝕰 𝕱 𝕲 𝕳 𝕴 𝕵 𝕶 𝕷 𝕸 𝕹 𝕺 𝕻 𝕼 𝕽 𝕾 𝕿 𝖀 𝖁 𝖂 𝖃 𝖄 𝖅 ! @ # $ % ^ & * ( ) ~ _ + | < > ? : " { }
GreekC	Α Β Χ Δ Ε Φ Γ Η Ι ϑ Κ Λ Μ Ν Ο Π Θ Ρ Σ Τ Τ ϒ Ω Ξ Ψ Ζ ! @ # $ % ^ & * ( ) ~ _ + | < > ? : " { }
GreekS	Α Β Χ Δ Ε Φ Γ Η Ι ϑ Κ Λ Μ Ν Ο Π Θ Ρ Σ Τ Τ ϒ Ω Ξ Ψ Ζ ! @ # $ % ^ & * ( ) ~ _ + | < > ? : " { }
IGES1001	A B C D E F G H I J K L M N O P Q R S T U V W X Y Z ! @ # $ % ~ & * ( ) ~ _ + | < > ? : " { }
IGES1002	A B C D E F G H I J K L M N O P Q R S T U V W X Y Z ! @ ± ˚ % ~ & * ( ) ⁻ _ + μ < > ? : " δ π
IGES1003	A B C D E F G H I J K L M N O P Q R S T U V W X Y Z ! @ # $ % ^ & * ( ) ˙ _ + | < > ? : " { }
Italic	*A B C D E F G H I J K L M N O P Q R S T U V W X Y Z ! @ # $ % ^ & * ( ) ~ _ + / < > ? : " { }*
Italic8	*A B C D E F G H I J K L M N O P Q R S T U V W X Y Z ! @ # $ % ^ & * ( ) ~ _ + / < > ? : " { }*
ItalicC	*A B C D E F G H I J K L M N O P Q R S T U V W X Y Z ! @ # $ % ^ & * ( ) ~ _ + / < > ? : " { }*
ItalicT	*A B C D E F G H I J K L M N O P Q R S T U V W X Y Z ! @ # $ % ^ & * ( ) ~ _ + / < > ? : " { }*
Monotxt	A B C D E F G H I J K L M N O P Q R S T U V W X Y Z ! @ # $ % ^ & * ( ) ~ _ + | < > ? ¡ ' ( )
RomanC	A B C D E F G H I J K L M N O P Q R S T U V W X Y Z ! @ # $ % ^ & * ( ) ~ _ + | < > ? : " { }
RomanD	A B C D E F G H I J K L M N O P Q R S T U V W X Y Z ! @ # $ % ^ & * ( ) ~ _ + | < > ? : " { }
RomanS	A B C D E F G H I J K L M N O P Q R S T U V W X Y Z ! @ # $ % ^ & * ( ) ~ _ + | < > ? : " { }
RomanT	A B C D E F G H I J K L M N O P Q R S T U V W X Y Z ! @ # $ % ^ & * ( ) ~ _ + | < > ? : " { }
ScriptC	*A B C D E F G H I J K L M N O P Q R S T U V W X Y Z ! @ # $ % ^ & * ( ) ~ _ + / < > ? : " { }*
ScriptS	*A B C D E F G H I J K L M N O P Q R S T U V W X Y Z ! @ # $ % ^ & * ( ) ~ _ + / < > ? : " { }*
Simplex	A B C D E F G H I J K L M N O P Q R S T U V W X Y Z ! @ # $ % ^ & * ( ) ~ _ + | < > ? : " { }
Syastro	☉ ☽ ☿ ♀ ⊕ ♂ ♃ ♄ ♅ Ψ ♇ ☊ ☋ ✳ ☌ ☋ ☍ ☉ ⋆ ♈ ♉ ♊ ♋ ♌ ♍ ♎ ♏ ♐ ♑ ♒ ♓ ! @ # $ % ~ & * ( ) ~ _ + | < > ? : " { }
Symap	○ □ △ ◇ ☆ + × ∗ ● ■ ▲ ◆ ▼ ▶ ▸ ⊢ ⊣ ⊥ ✳ ✚ ⊹ ◐ ◑ ○ ○ △! @ # $ % ~ & * ( ) ~ _ + | < > ? : " { }
Symath	ℵ ′ | || ± ∓ × · ÷ = ≠ ≡ < > ≦ ≧ ∝ ~ √ C ∪ ⊃ ∩ ∈ → ↑ ! @ # $ % ~ & * ( ) ~ _ + | < > ? : " { }
Symeteo	· · · · ▲ ● ▲ ^ ^ ∩ ∪ ‿ ﹍ ﹏ ﹏ S ~ ∞ R δ ⟋ ╲ ─ ╱ ! @ # $ % ~ & * ( ) ~ _ + | < > ? : " { }
Symusic	· ‧ ⸲ ♪ o o ● # ♮ ♭ ⁻ ⁻ × ⌐ 𝄞 ℗ 𝄡 · ⁃ ── ∧ ⇌ ! @ # $ % ^ & * ( ) ~ _ + | < > ? : " { }
Txt	A B C D E F G H I J K L M N O P Q R S T U V W X Y Z ! @ # $ % ^ & * ( ) ~ _ + | < > ? ¡ ' ( )

Complex	a b c d e f g h i j k l mn o p q r s t u v w x y z 1 2 3 4 5 6 7 8 9 0 ` - = \ , . / ; ' [ ]
GothicE	a b c d e f g h i j k l mn o p q r s t u v w x y z 1 2 3 4 5 6 7 8 9 0 ` - = \ , . / ; ' [ ]
GothicG	a b c d e f g h i j t l mn o p q r f t u v w x y z 1 2 3 4 5 6 7 8 9 0 ` - = \ , . / ; ' [ ]
GothicI	a b c d e f g h i j k l mn o p q r s t u v w x y z 1 2 3 4 5 6 7 8 9 0 ` - = \ , . / ; ' [ ]
GreekC	α β χ δ ε φ γ η ι ∂ κ λ μ ν ο π ϑ ρ σ τ υ ∈ ω ξ ψ ζ 1 2 3 4 5 6 7 8 9 0 ` - = \ , . / ; ' [ ]
GreekS	α β χ δ ε φ γ η ι ∂ κ λ μ ν ο π ϑ ρ σ τ υ ∈ ω ξ ψ ζ 1 2 3 4 5 6 7 8 9 0 ` - = \ , . / ; ' [ ]
IGES1001	∠ Φ ▱ ⌂ ○ // ∅ ≣ ⊕ ⌐ ⊛ Ø ○ ⊙ ⊗ ☐ ○ △ ◇ ⟁ ☒ Υ 1 2 3 4 5 6 7 8 9 0 ` - = \ , . / ; ' [ ]
IGES1002	℧ ✛ ≤ ≥ Δ ✓ × ≡ ≠ ∫ ⊃ ∪ ∧ ≈ Σ ↑ ↓ → ← φ θ γ ψ ω λ α 1 2 3 4 5 6 7 8 9 0 ` - = \ , . / ; ' [ ]
IGES1003	∠ ⊥ ▱ ⌂ ○ // ∅ ≣ ⊕ ∩ ⊛ ⊕ Ø ○ ⊙ ⊗ ☐ ⌐ ⌐ ∨ ⟁ ✦ ⊾ 1 2 3 4 5 6 7 8 9 0 ` - = \ , . / ; ' [ ]
Italic	a b c d e f g h i j k l mn o p q r s t u v w x y z 1 2 3 4 5 6 7 8 9 0 ` - = \ , . / ; ' [ ]
Italic8	a b c d e f g h i j k l mn o p q r s t u v w x y z 1 2 3 4 5 6 7 8 9 0 ` - = \ , . / ; ' [ ]
ItalicC	a b c d e f g h i j k l mn o p q r s t u v w x y z 1 2 3 4 5 6 7 8 9 0 ` - = \ , . / ; ' [ ]
ItalicT	a b c d e f g h i j k l mn o p q r s t u v w x y z 1 2 3 4 5 6 7 8 9 0 ` - = \ , . / ; ' [ ]
Monotxt	a b c d e f g h i j k l m n o p q r s t u v w x y z 1 2 3 4 5 6 7 8 9 0 ` - = \ , . / ; ' [ ]
RomanC	a b c d e f g h i j k l mn o p q r s t u v w x y z 1 2 3 4 5 6 7 8 9 0 ` - = \ , . / ; ' [ ]
RomanD	a b c d e f g h i j k l mn o p q r s t u v w x y z 1 2 3 4 5 6 7 8 9 0 ` - = \ , . / ; ' [ ]
RomanS	a b c d e f g h i j k l mn o p q r s t u v w x y z 1 2 3 4 5 6 7 8 9 0 ` - = \ , . / ; ' [ ]
RomanT	a b c d e f g h i j k l mn o p q r s t u v w x y z 1 2 3 4 5 6 7 8 9 0 ` - = \ , . / ; ' [ ]
ScriptC	a b c d e f g h i j k l mn o p q r s t u v w x y z 1 2 3 4 5 6 7 8 9 0 ` - = \ , . / ; ' [ ]
ScriptS	a b c d e f g h i j k l mn o p q r s t u v w x y z 1 2 3 4 5 6 7 8 9 0 ` - = \ , . / ; ' [ ]
Simplex	a b c d e f g h i j k l mn o p q r s t u v w x y z 1 2 3 4 5 6 7 8 9 0 ` - = \ , . / ; ' [ ]
Syastro	✳ ✱ ' ⌣ ∪ ∩ ∈ → ↑ ← ↓ ∂ ∇ ^ ˘ ˘ ℵ § † ‡ ∃ ℒ ⊕ © 1 2 3 4 5 6 7 8 9 0 ` - = \ , . / ; ' [ ]
Symap	♀ ♣ ♁ ♡ ◦ · · ○ ○ ○ ◯ ◯ ◯ ⬭ ⊓ ⊥ ∴ ∴ ♤ ♢ ◇ ✦ ♠ ♣ 1 2 3 4 5 6 7 8 9 0 ` - = \ , . / ; ' [ ]
Symath	← ↓ ∂ ∇ √ ∫ ∮ ∞ § † ‡ ∃ ∏ Σ ( ) [ ] { } { } ∫ ∫ √ ∫ ≈ ≅ 1 2 3 4 5 6 7 8 9 0 = \ , . / ; [ ]
Symeteo	│ \ ˜ ˊ ¦ ˋ ⌣ ⌣ ⤙ ( ) ⤳ ⋏ ⋏ ⋔ Ω α τ ⊌ ⊍ φ φ • 1 2 3 4 5 6 7 8 9 0 = \ , . / ; [ ]
Symusic	· ˏ ♪ ○ ○ ● ♯ ♮ ♭ ⌐ ⌐ ↰ ↱ 𝄞 𝄢 𝄡 ⊙ ♀ ♀ ⊕ ♂ ♃ ♄ ♅ Ψ ♭ 1 2 3 4 5 6 7 8 9 0 ` ¯ = \ , . / ; [ ]
Txt	a b c d e f g h i j k l mn o p q r s t u v w x y z 1 2 3 4 5 6 7 8 9 0 ` - = \ , . / ; ' [ ]

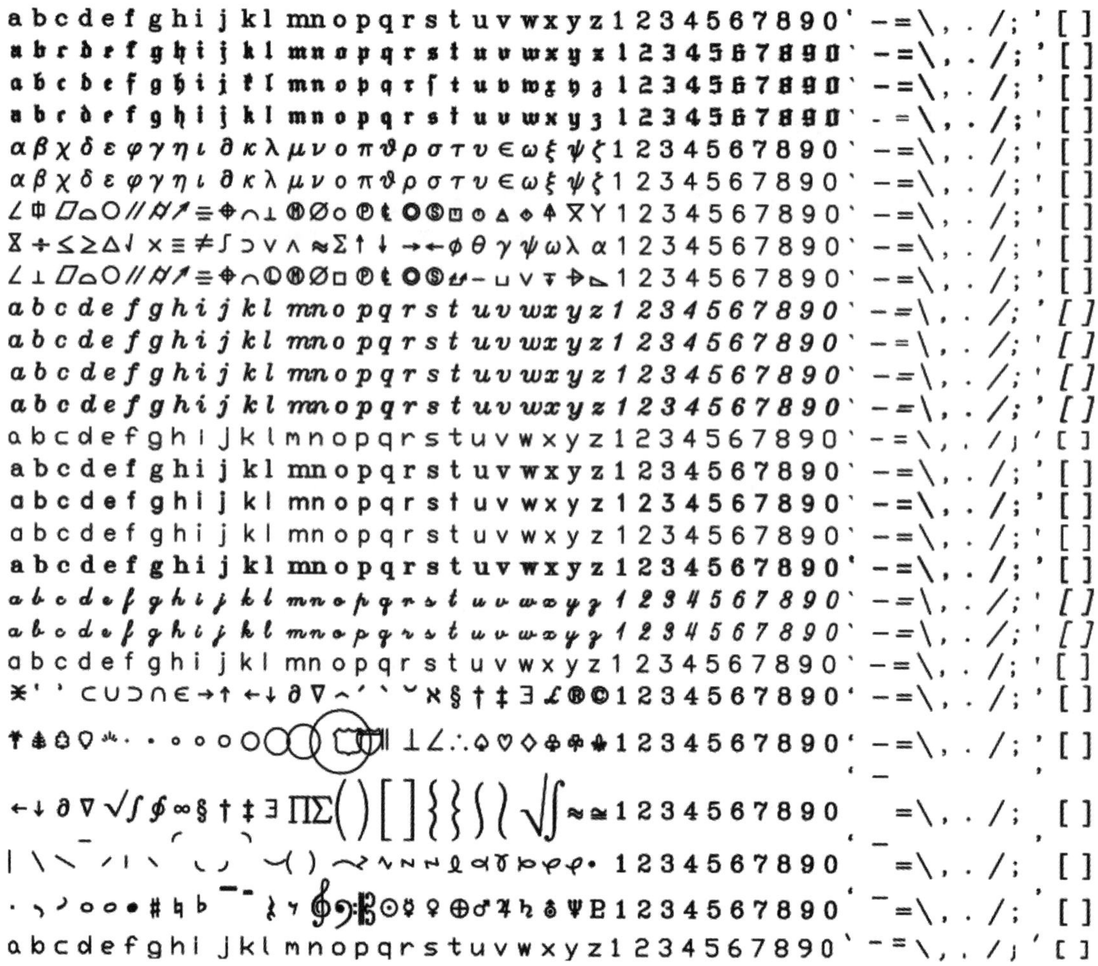

Configuration Issues with AutoCAD

There are a few basic parameters which AutoCAD uses to determine the format and style of some of the displays you will see as you are working with AutoCAD. This appendix will explain some of the parameters which may need to be changed to get results as shown in the text. This is not an exhaustive list of all parameters, but will discuss the more common ones. To change a parameter, simply type the parameter name at the command line and AutoCAD will request a new value.

Parameter	Suggested Value	AutoCAD Default	Description
STARTUPTODAY	0	1	Controls the initial startup dialog box. A value of 0 is less confusing for a beginning student and is the format used in compiling this text.
CURSORSIZE	100	5	Controls the size of the crosshairs. The value is the percent of the screen which the crosshairs cover.
UCSFOLLOW	0	0	Controls whether a new viewpoint is created to yield a plan view every time a new coordinate system is created.
WORLDVIEW	1	1	All viewpoints are relative to the World Coordinate System.
DIMASSOC	2	2	Controls the format used when dimensioning.
EXPERT	0	0	Controls the level of messages shown. A setting of zero shows all messages.
FILEDIA	1	1	Controls the display of dialog boxes for file input/output.
CMDDIA	1	1	Will suppress some dialog boxes in favor of command line input.
PICKFIRST	1	1	Will allow pre-selection of objects using grips.
UCSICON	0 – for 2D 3 – for 3D	3	Controls whether the UCSICON will be displayed and where. Zero is not displayed, three is displayed at the origin.

Creation of Template Files

The creation of a template file in AutoCAD is nothing more than the creation of a drawing file. Once the file is created, rather than simply saving it, you must use the "Save As" option and change the file type from "AutoCAD 2007 Format" to "AutoCAD Drawing Template." This will default to your template file directory. Your template file can contain any setting you want to include and subsequent drawings created from this template as well as any entities you want to be present in those drawings. These entities are typically elements like a border, title block, or company logo. The remainder of this appendix will be devoted to discussing some of the basic settings which should be considered in the creation of a template file.

Layers

By default AutoCAD has only a layer named "0" available. To create additional layers you should use the command LAYER or select the icon to the left of the layer name in the properties toolbar. The resulting dialog box, shown in Figure A4.1, can be used to add or delete layers and establish the properties (color, line weight, line type) for the layer. Once you have all the layers you will need, select the OK button to dismiss the box.

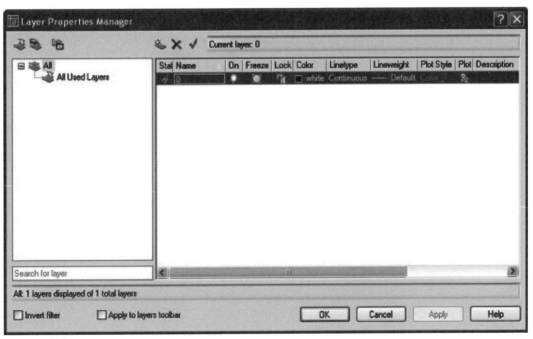

Figure A4.1

Styles

Text styles should be established for your drawings. You can either redefine the standard text style called "STANDARD" or create a new style. Also Dimensioning Styles should be set up to accommodate future needs.

Basic Settings

Some basic settings also need to be established. These have been discussed through the book. In particular you should consider the following:

DIMASSOC

UCSICON

GRID

SNAP

LIMITS

LTSCALE

CELTSCALE

INDEX